I0835599

KNOW THYSELF

THE LIGHT WITHIN

ARWIN VALENCIA, MD

Copyright Notice

ANG POWER PUBLISHING HOUSE
PO BOX 10735 / Glendale, CA 91209-USA
ANGPowerPHouse@Gmail.com
ISBN: 978-1-966837-22-0

Printed in the United States of America

To all fellow sojourners of the soul,

May our paths be illuminated by truth,
guided by love, and anchored
in the light within.

Know Thyself, The Light Within

Know thyself, a sacred call,
Beyond the noise, beyond the wall.
In deep silence, the truth begins—
You are the Light that dwells within.

Not just a name, or skin, or role,
But endless fire, an ageless soul.
The world's illusion fades and thins,
Revealing stillness deep within.

Each joy and sorrow, gain and loss,
Leads you closer to the cross—
Where ego dies and truth can spin
The golden thread that lies within.

The mirror shows a fleeting face,
But not the Light, nor timeless grace.
Close your eyes, let peace begin—
And feel the pulse that shines within.

No need to chase the stars afar,
You are already what they are.
Each breath a bridge, each step akin
To finding home—the path is within.

Let go of fear, release the shame,
You are not broken, nor to blame.
You are the calm amidst the din—
You are the Love that flows within.

So, know thyself, and you shall see
The Light you seek is what you be.
No greater truth has ever been—
Than this: You are the Light within.

MysticSojourn66

"The privilege of a lifetime is to become who you truly are."

Carl Jung

Song of the Soul

In the depth of my soul there is
A wordless song - a song that lives
In the seed of my heart.
It refuses to melt with ink on
Parchment: it engulfs my affection
In a transparent cloak and flows,
But not upon my lips.

How can I sigh it? I fear it may
Mingle with earthly ether.
To whom shall I sing it? It dwells
In the house of my soul, in fear of
Harsh ears.

When I look into my inner eyes
I see the shadow of its shadow.
When I touch my fingertips
I feel its vibrations.

The deeds of my hands heed its
Presence as a lake must reflect
The glittering stars; my tears
Reveal it, as bright drops of dew
Reveal the secret of a withering rose.

It is a song composed by contemplation,
And published by silence,
And shunned by clamor,
And folded by truth,
And repeated by dreams,

And understood by love,
And hidden by awakening,
And sung by the soul.

It is the song of love.
What Cain or Esau could sing it?
It is more fragrant than jasmine.
What voice could enslave it?
It is heart bound, as a virgin's secret.
What string could quiver it?

Who dares unite the roar of the sea
And the singing of the nightingale?
Who dares compare the shrieking tempest.

To the sigh of an infant?
Who dares speak aloud the words
Intended for the heart to speak?
What human dares sing in voice
The song of God?

Kahlil Gibran

Table of Contents

Introduction: A Journey of Remembering

"The longest journey you will ever take is the journey inward."

Navajo Proverb

We live in a world bustling with information, saturated with distractions, and driven by a restless pursuit for validation, success, and belonging. Amid this whirlwind of modern life, we are led to believe that the answers to life's most profound questions lie somewhere "out there"—in doctrines, achievements, relationships, or external authorities. We search endlessly for purpose, peace, power, and love, often unaware that what we truly seek has always resided within.

This book, *Know Thyself: The Light Within*, is an invitation to journey inward—to rediscover the radiant essence that exists at the core of your being. It is a call to awaken from the illusion of separation and limitation and to remember the truth that has been quietly whispering from the depths of your soul: **You are not broken. You are not lost. You are not merely human. You are a spark of the Divine in human form.**

This work is not a typical self-help manual, nor is it a spiritual doctrine bound by religion. It is a tapestry woven from the threads of science and spirituality, psychology and mysticism, personal reflection and universal truth. It is a soul-centered map guiding you back to your inner wholeness—a remembrance that healing, transformation, and true freedom begin not in controlling the outer world, but in illuminating the world within.

Why This Book, Why Now?

We are at a pivotal moment in human evolution. Collectively, we are awakening from a deep slumber—emerging from centuries of identification with ego, fear, and illusion. The structures of the old paradigm are crumbling. What once served us—rigid systems, power hierarchies, external authority, even aspects of organized religion—is no longer enough to meet the hunger of the soul. The soul does not seek control; it seeks truth. It does not seek comfort; it seeks expansion.

The call to "know thyself" is not merely philosophical. It is existential. In a world facing global instability, moral ambiguity, and a crisis of meaning, the most revolutionary act is to awaken to who you truly are. To shed the false self, to break free from societal conditioning, and to stand in the clarity of your soul's essence.

As a physician, I have witnessed the fragility of life and the resilience of the human spirit. As a spiritual seeker, I have journeyed through the winding roads of belief, doubt, surrender, and revelation. And as a soul, I have come to understand that beneath the roles we play and the wounds we carry, there is a sacred light within us all—a light not of this world, but the very source of it.

The Layers of Forgetting

At birth, we arrive with open hearts and pure awareness. But as we grow, we are taught what to believe, how to behave, who to be. We are rewarded for conformity and punished for authenticity. We adapt by layering our inner light with masks of identity—race, gender, nationality, occupation, religion. We inherit unresolved traumas, cultural programming, and ancestral pain. We forget our divine origin and begin to live from the outside-in rather than the inside-out.

This forgetting is not failure; it is the human curriculum. We are not here by accident. Each of us chose to incarnate at this time, to participate in the great dance of remembering. And the forgetting serves a sacred purpose: to give us the opportunity to choose love, to rediscover our light in the darkest of places, and to expand consciousness through embodied experience.

You Are Not Your Thoughts

One of the first keys to awakening is this: *You are not your thoughts.*

Thoughts are tools of the mind—useful, powerful, but not inherently true. The mind creates narratives, judgments, and identities, but it is the observer behind the thoughts who is real. That silent witness, that still presence, is the eternal you. The ego is a necessary interface for living in this world, but it must remain the servant, not the master. When the ego runs the show, we become trapped in survival consciousness—seeking control, approval, and certainty. But when we reclaim our seat as the observer, we begin to live from a deeper intelligence, one rooted in soul, not story.

The Power of Vibration and Frequency

Everything in the universe is energy. Every thought, emotion, belief, and action carry a frequency. We attract into our lives what matches our dominant energetic signature. This is not mystical fluff—it is quantum law. Understanding this truth empowers us to shift from victims of circumstance to conscious co-creators of our reality.

When we operate in fear, shame, guilt, or anger, we emit lower frequencies and invite chaos, stagnation, or pain. When we align with love, gratitude, joy, and compassion, we vibrate at higher frequencies and magnetize synchronicity, peace, and abundance. To "know thyself" is to become the steward of your own vibration—consciously tending to the garden of your inner world.

The Healing Path: Integration, Not Perfection

Many believe healing is about becoming flawless, pure, or enlightened. But healing is not the absence of wounds—it is the integration of them. It is the alchemy of turning pain into purpose, trauma into wisdom, and shadows into light. Wholeness is not perfection; it is acceptance.

Kintsugi, the Japanese art of repairing broken pottery with gold, teaches us that the cracks are not to be hidden but honored. In the same way, our wounds become sacred entry points through which grace can enter. Every heartbreak, every failure, every disappointment is not a detour from your path—it *is* the path. Healing is not about erasing the past but about reclaiming your light from it.

Divine Timing and the Mystery of Surrender

We live in a culture obsessed with control, outcomes, and deadlines. Yet life unfolds not on our terms, but in divine timing. The soul's journey cannot be rushed. What appears as delay is often preparation. What feels like failure is often redirection. Surrender is not weakness—it is trust. It is the willingness to release the illusion of control and allow life to lead you to where your soul longs to be.

True power lies not in manipulation but in surrender. When we let go of needing to know how, when, or where, we open the door for miracles. Surrender aligns us with flow, with grace, with destiny—not as a fixed outcome, but as a frequency we can embody.

Sacred Boundaries and the Sovereignty of the Soul

As we awaken, we become more sensitive to energy. Not all people or environments serve our expansion. This is where sacred boundaries become essential—not to isolate ourselves, but to honor the light within. Boundaries are not walls; they are thresholds. They are declarations of self-respect, invitations for mutual honor, and containers for authentic connection.

To know thyself is to reclaim your sovereignty—to stop outsourcing your worth, your voice, or your truth. You are not here to live someone else's script. You are here to express your soul's unique note in the symphony of existence.

From Emotion to Essence: Love as a Frequency

Love is often mistaken as a fleeting emotion tied to conditions and attachments. But true love—divine love—is a state of being, a frequency that emanates from the very fabric of creation. Love without attachment, service without expectation; these are not moral ideals, but energetic truths.

When we live in this frequency, we no longer grasp or beg for love; we become it. We radiate it.

This is not naïve spirituality. This is embodied wisdom. The more we embody love, the more we transmute fear. The more we forgive, the more we free ourselves. The more we serve from wholeness, the more we fulfill our soul's purpose.

Synchronicity and the Orchestration of the Universe

Coincidences are not random; they are spiritual breadcrumbs guiding us home. When we begin to awaken, we notice patterns, signs, and synchronicities that defy logic. These are winks from the universe—reminders that we are seen, supported, and deeply interconnected. The more aligned we become with our authentic frequency, the more these synchronicities accelerate. Life becomes a dance, a dialogue, a sacred choreography.

To "know thyself" is to develop the eyes to see behind the veil of coincidence. It is to recognize that everything is energy, everything is connected, and everything is part of a greater unfolding.

The Invitation of This Book

Each chapter in this book is a mirror—reflecting different aspects of your divine essence and your human journey. Some chapters may challenge you. Others may soothe you. All are designed to awaken you to the truth that you are more than a body, more than a role, more than a mind. You are a soul, here on purpose, guided by a deeper intelligence that is always calling you home.

This book offers:

- Reflections on energy, vibration, and the quantum field of consciousness
- Insights into identity, ego, trauma, and the journey of self-reclamation
- Explorations of divine timing, destiny, surrender, and intuition
- Practices for raising your frequency and becoming a conscious creator
- Gentle but powerful reminders that healing is possible, wholeness is real, and love is your true nature

You may read this book sequentially or let your intuition guide you to the chapter you need most in the moment. However, you move through it, may each word be a lantern illuminating your path inward.

A Final Word: Awakening the Light Within

You were never meant to merely survive. You were born to shine.

The light you seek is not in the stars or scriptures—it is in your own being. You are the temple, the priest, the flame, and the offering. The Divine is not separate from you. It pulses in your breath, sings through your heartbeat, and dreams through your desires.

To *know thyself* is to awaken from the illusion of separation and remember your sacred origin. It is to claim your life not as a random occurrence, but as a divine appointment. You are here not just to exist—but to illuminate, to heal, to remember, and to love.

This is the journey of a lifetime. This is the journey of the soul. And it begins right here, right now—with the choice to go within.

Chapter 1

To Seek God Is to Stop Running from Yourself

You search the skies, you roam the seas,
In temples, books, and ancient trees.
You chase a voice, a sacred sound,
Yet what you seek is inward bound.

You wear a mask, you play the part,
But Truth still waits within your heart.
No need to flee, no need to roam—
The path to God leads you back home.

So, pause the race, remove disguise,
And see the soul behind your eyes.
The One you seek, the silent guide,
Has never left—just dwells inside.

In a world filled with trials and tribulations, it's easy to feel as though we are at the mercy of forces beyond our control—subject to divine whims that dictate whether we fail or succeed. Many resign themselves to fate, adopting a passive stance in the unfolding of their own lives. This surrender to external forces is not only disempowering—it is a subtle form of escapism. By avoiding responsibility and refusing to actively shape our own reality, we deny our true nature and forfeit the gift of self-agency.

Beliefs, superstitions, and even institutionalized religion have long encouraged this mindset. Deeply embedded in both personal psyche and collective consciousness, these ideologies often dictate what is acceptable, moral, or "divinely approved." Cultural expectations and familial traditions reinforce this conformity. To question them is considered taboo—sacrilegious even—and doing so can threaten our sense of identity and belonging. Faced with the choice to either conform or diverge, many opt for the former, finding comfort in collective obedience rather than venturing into the unknown.

Yet no matter how tightly we cling to inherited systems of belief, there emerges—sooner or later—a whisper from within. This inner voice questions the constructs we've accepted without examination. It beckons us not outward, but inward. At first, we may seek answers externally—through doctrines, rituals, or spiritual authorities—but the deeper the longing, the clearer the realization: the only path to truth is within. The journey toward self-realization inevitably turns us inward, where the divine is not an entity separate from us but the very essence of who we are.

As Rumi so eloquently expressed, "You are not a drop in the ocean. You are the entire ocean in a drop." This quote beautifully dismantles the illusion of separation. We are not fragmented beings hoping to reconnect with a distant God—we are divine consciousness experiencing itself in human form. The limitations, fears, and perceived failures we encounter are not punishments or trials imposed by an external judge; they are elements of a game we chose to play in this 3D reality. It is up to us to either remain trapped in that illusion or awaken, rewrite the rules, and reclaim our sovereignty.

The notion of an external God—distant, judgmental, and appeased only through obedience—is part of that illusion. It keeps us in fear, encouraging dependence and perpetuating the myth of our own inadequacy. In truth, we are not powerless; we are simply afraid of what it means to fully embrace our power. Fear fosters a reptilian mindset—one rooted in scarcity, separation, and survival. And so, we run—from our pain, from our past, from our true selves—hiding behind distractions, drama, and complexity.

But spiritual awakening begins when we stop running. "To seek God is to stop running from yourself" is more than a poetic assertion—it is a spiritual imperative. To truly seek God is to turn inward, to face the shadows we've long avoided: our insecurities, regrets, traumas, and fears. It is to meet ourselves with radical honesty and compassion, to strip away the personas we've adopted for acceptance, and to encounter the naked truth of who we are.

This is not an act of self-condemnation, but of divine remembrance. In seeking God within, we discover strength, forgiveness, and unconditional love. We begin to recognize that the Divine was never separate from us. It was hidden in plain sight—in the quiet moments of self-reflection, in the ache of longing, in the courage to forgive, and in the peace that comes from embracing the whole of who we are.

Reflective Conclusion

To seek God is not to escape this world or ascend beyond the self—it is to descend fully into your own depths, to stop running, and to come home to your soul. It is the brave act of standing still in your own presence and seeing that what you've been chasing all along is already within you. In that stillness, the illusion of separation dissolves, and what remains is truth: You are not just seeking God. You are remembering that you are already divine.

Chapter 2

Truth: Not Learned but Remembered

Not carved in stone, nor taught in school,
But whispered deep, where silence rules.
Beyond the facts the mind can find,
Truth waits within the quiet mind.

Not learned through books or outward quest,
But stirred awake in inner rest.
A voice that calls with ancient grace—
A soul's own echo, time can't erase.

No map can guide, no chart can show,
The path to truths we already know.
For what we seek, we've always known—
Truth is the seed we call our own.

Truth, in its simplest form, is that which accurately reflects reality. It is the alignment between what is perceived and what is. Philosophically, this understanding is rooted in the correspondence theory of truth, which states that a belief or statement is true if it corresponds with a fact. For example, the claim "The sky is blue" is considered true if it indeed matches the observable color of the sky.

While objective truth aligns with external reality, human experience adds complexity to its definition. We often distinguish between **objective truth** (verifiable and fact-based), **subjective truth** (based on personal perception),

normative truth (what we ought to do, often shaped by cultural and moral frameworks), and **positive truth** (a form of uplifting belief rooted in hope or spiritual trust).

Subjective truths are born from personal experience — how we interpret events, emotions, or relationships. They are valid not because they are universal, but because they are sincerely lived. In contrast, normative truths arise from societal standards, moral traditions, or ethical teachings and help form the blueprint of collective living. Positive truth transcends mere fact or logic; it uplifts, comforts, and guides, especially during moments of struggle. These truths do not necessarily rely on empirical evidence but offer emotional or spiritual sustenance.

Then there is **spiritual truth**, which defies the bounds of logic and empirical data. It speaks to a deeper knowing — not of the intellect but of the soul. Spiritual truth concerns itself with the nature of consciousness, the presence of a higher power, the journey of the soul, and the interconnectedness of all life. It is often accessed not through study but through inner stillness, faith, intuition, or divine revelation. Spiritual truths transcend observable facts and dwell in the sacred — offering us meaning, direction, and the remembrance of who we truly are.

Plato's theory of *anamnesis*, or recollection, elegantly illustrates this idea. In his dialogues, particularly in *Meno* and *Phaedo*, Plato suggests that the soul existed before birth and had already encountered eternal truths. Learning, then, is not the acquisition of something new but the *remembering* of what the soul already knows. This philosophy finds resonance in spiritual teachings across cultures: enlightenment or awakening is not about becoming something new — it is about peeling away the layers of illusion to rediscover the truth that has always been within us.

This is the core of many spiritual awakenings: they are not external revelations but internal remembrances. We remember our true essence, our divine nature, and the sacred purpose for which we came to Earth. That's why no two awakenings look the same — each soul carries a unique frequency, a specific mission, and a personal path of return to truth. There is no universal roadmap, only the inner compass of intuition and soul-knowing.

Awakening, in this context, is less about reaching for something outside ourselves and more about quieting the noise, shedding false identities, and coming home to the wisdom already etched in our being. The difficulty lies not in the absence of truth, but in trusting ourselves enough to hear it — to believe in that quiet voice within even when it contradicts the world around us.

Reflective Conclusion

Truth, ultimately, is not something we acquire like a possession — it is something we *remember*. It lives in the quiet recesses of the soul, waiting for us to awaken to its presence. Objective truths ground us in reality, subjective truths color our perception, and spiritual truths anchor us in eternal knowing.

In a world that often demands proof, the deeper truths whisper gently: "You already know." The journey of remembering is sacred, personal, and transformative. It invites us to release the noise of the world and tune into the silent knowing of our own soul. In doing so, we do not just learn — we *remember* who we are, why we are here, and the eternal truths that have always been ours to reclaim.

Chapter 3

Wholeness Is Found in the Broken Pieces

The cracks you hide, the wounds you bear,
Are golden seams beyond compare.
Not flaws, but maps where light breaks through—
The art of healing shaping you.

Each shattered piece, a sacred part,
Restored by grace, refined by heart.
You're not less whole for what you've lost—
You've found your soul, no matter the cost.

In the heart of every soul lies a deep yearning for wholeness. We seek a sense of completeness, a life unfractured, stable, and full. Yet, the very nature of our earthly existence is one of change, unpredictability, and imperfection. In this constantly shifting world, we often find ourselves broken in ways we never anticipated—by loss, disappointment, betrayal, failure, or grief. And while we cannot control the external variables that life presents, we *can* choose how we relate to them. Our perspective, our response, and our willingness to grow through hardship ultimately shape the path toward authentic wholeness.

Paradoxically, no one arrives at a state of genuine wholeness without first being broken. It is in our shattered moments—

when life strips away our illusions, our expectations, and even parts of our identity—that we encounter the raw truth of our being. These moments humble us, awaken us, and offer us an invitation: not to return to what we were, but to rebuild into something far more enduring, integrated, and wise.

To be human is to give parts of ourselves to others and to the world. In loving, serving, and sacrificing, we offer fragments of our inner being for the sake of something greater. But just as we pour ourselves out, life invites us to reclaim these scattered pieces—not to return to a former self, but to reassemble them into a new form of wholeness: one shaped by experience, resilience, and sacred transformation.

The Japanese art of **Kintsugi** offers a powerful metaphor for this process. Kintsugi—literally translated as *"golden joinery"*—is the ancient practice of repairing broken pottery with lacquer mixed with powdered gold, silver, or platinum. Rather than disguising the cracks, this art form *highlights* them, honoring the history of the object and elevating its brokenness into something beautiful, unique, and more valuable than before.

Kintsugi embodies the philosophy of *wabi-sabi*, which embraces the beauty of imperfection, impermanence, and incompleteness. It teaches us that what is broken is not ruined; it is *transformed*. The damage doesn't diminish the object's worth—it becomes the very story that makes it special. The golden seams, far from being flaws, become sacred scars of survival and strength.

In the same way, our personal brokenness can be seen not as failure or deficiency, but as an essential part of our soul's journey. When we surrender to the healing process—when we allow grace, time, and self-compassion to mend the fractured parts of our being—something extraordinary happens. We become more authentic. More open. More connected to others and to our divine essence.

Through this lens, being broken is not an end—it is an initiation. A breaking open, not apart. Often, the cracks in our lives are the very channels through which grace flows. As the poet and mystic Rumi once said, *"The wound is the place where the light enters you."*

What It Truly Means to Be Whole

- **Embracing Imperfection:**
  Wholeness does not mean perfection. It means embracing every aspect of yourself—especially the broken ones—as integral to who you are becoming.

- **Discovering Purpose Through Pain:**
  Brokenness often awakens new levels of empathy, purpose, and inner wisdom that would have remained dormant otherwise.

- **Fostering Growth and Resilience:**
  Every crack tells a story of strength. Every repair is a testament to your capacity to rise, rebuild, and evolve.

- **Letting the Light In:**

Our vulnerabilities allow deeper connection—not just with

others, but with the divine spark within ourselves.

- **Experiencing Spiritual Transformation:**

  Many spiritual traditions affirm that brokenness is a necessary part of creation. From the chaos of collapse comes the clarity of rebirth.

Reflective Conclusion

The Sacred Art of Becoming

"Wholeness is found in broken pieces" is not just a poetic phrase—it is a truth echoed across the soul's journey. The life you are living now, with all its cracks and fractures, is not evidence of failure. It is the raw material of your transformation. Your pain holds the blueprint for your evolution. Your scars are not shameful—they are sacred.

True wholeness is not about restoring what was, but allowing what is to be reshaped by love, wisdom, and divine intention. Like a vessel repaired with gold, you are not just mended—you are *transfigured.* Stronger, richer, and more radiant than before.

So, honor your cracks. Cherish your fragments. And know this: You were never truly broken—only being prepared for the masterpiece you were always meant to become.

Chapter 4

Embrace the Contrast. It Reveals the Light

In light we dance, in dark we grow,
Through highs and lows, the soul will know.
Each contrast carves a deeper way,
To birth the truth, we hide each day.

The night reveals the stars above,
Just as pain reveals our love.
Embrace it all—both joy and strife,
For contrast is the art of life.

The governing principle of this earthly reality is duality—a realm where everything exists in pairs of opposites. Light and darkness. Joy and suffering. Love and hate. Order and chaos. These polarities shape the very fabric of our existence, creating a dynamic landscape through which we, as sentient beings, journey and evolve.

Every day, we navigate this realm of contrast, often choosing which end of the spectrum to align ourselves with. Yet not all experiences come by choice. Sometimes, we are thrust into circumstances beyond our control—unexpected hardships, emotional turbulence, loss, or sudden transformations. These are the uninvited contrasts that life delivers, testing our capacity to remain grounded, aware, and compassionate.

As conscious beings—endowed with the ability to think, feel, and reflect—we are not mere bystanders in this dance of opposites. We are participants, creators, and observers all at once. Our emotional responses, relationships, and inner worlds are continually shaped by our interaction with these opposing forces. And it is precisely through these interactions that we come to know ourselves more deeply.

From a metaphysical and spiritual perspective, we are more than physical form. At our core, we are photonic beings—emanations of pure Divine light—who have willingly chosen to experience existence within the constraints of form. To enter the world of limitation, density, and separation. In doing so, we allow our light to pass through the prism of 3D reality, splitting into countless rays of experience: joy, pain, beauty, sorrow, triumph, and loss. Each of these rays carries a unique vibrational frequency, painting a multidimensional canvas of contrast.

Darkness as a Canvas for Light

Just as a single beam of light becomes visible and meaningful only when cast against the backdrop of darkness, so too do our moments of inner light—our triumphs, joys, and awakenings—become truly appreciated only in the presence of shadow. In a completely lit room, light may go unnoticed. But in darkness, even the faintest flicker becomes profound. So too in life, our growth and gratitude often emerge from the depths of hardship.

Struggles, when embraced with awareness, reveal our resilience. They uncover hidden strengths and call forth courage we didn't know we had. It is through pain that we learn compassion, through loneliness that we understand connection, and through loss that we come to treasure presence.

The Path to Healing

The invitation, then, is not to flee from the dark or deny its existence, but to meet it with grace. When we confront our shadows—our fears, insecurities, and wounds—we begin the sacred work of alchemy: transforming pain into wisdom and suffering into light. This journey toward healing requires radical honesty and deep trust in the intelligence of the soul's unfolding.

In many spiritual traditions, darkness is associated with ignorance, illusion, or separation from the Divine, while light represents truth, clarity, and divine presence. But rather than demonizing one and glorifying the other, we are called to recognize the necessity of both. Without darkness, light cannot be known. Without descent, there can be no ascent. Light becomes meaningful only because darkness exists.

Reflective Conclusion

The Gift of Contrast: To *embrace the contrast* is to recognize that life, in its fullness, includes both valleys and peaks, both sorrow and ecstasy. It is to understand that our soul did not incarnate to avoid difficulty but to grow through it. Each contrast serves as a sacred teacher, revealing new facets of our divinity and guiding us back to the truth of who we are.

The duality of life is not a punishment—it is a purposeful design. Through contrast, we remember our light. Through brokenness, we rediscover wholeness. Through separation, we awaken to oneness. And in embracing all that life presents—light and shadow alike—we align more deeply with the Divine presence that lives within us.

So, do not fear the dark. Do not resist the storm. For every contrast you encounter is a mirror, reflecting your light more clearly. Embrace it all, and in doing so, you will come to embody the radiance you've always carried within.

Chapter 5

Reality is a Choice: Nothing Around You is Real Until You Decide It Is

Nothing is real 'til you choose it to be,
A thought, a dream, a silent decree.
The world reflects your inner tone,
What you claim is what is shown.

Not by force, nor desperate plea,
But calm alignment sets you free.
Decide with heart, not fear or strife—
And watch your choice become your life.

Our reality is not something imposed upon us; rather, it is something we co-create through the lens of our perception, the frequency of our vibration, and the choices we make—both consciously and unconsciously. The statement *"Nothing around you is real until you decide it is"* may sound abstract or mystical, yet it encapsulates a profound truth grounded in both spiritual insight and quantum thought.

We are vibrational beings living in a vibrational universe. Everything we experience is a mirror reflecting our inner state of consciousness. When we dwell in peace, harmony, and clarity, we attract external circumstances that echo those frequencies. Conversely, when we reside in fear, anxiety, or unworthiness, those vibrations shape the world we perceive and experience.

This is the essence of the Law of Attraction—not just a popular phrase, but a description of how resonance works in the quantum field. Every potential version of our life already exists in the realm of possibilities. These possibilities are not accessed through desperation, need, or mere wishful thinking, but through energetic alignment. We manifest not by chasing outcomes but by becoming energetically congruent with what we seek.

Yet, alignment often feels elusive. Why? Because many of us are unconsciously programmed with beliefs rooted in fear, scarcity, and limitation. These patterns often stem from generational trauma, cultural conditioning, or deeply buried emotional wounds stored in the subconscious. As a result, we engage with life through automatic, reactive responses—reflexes formed not from conscious intention but from embedded programming.

Paradoxically, it is often easier to manifest what we *don't* want because those unconscious beliefs vibrate more consistently with our internal state. Lack, fear, and resistance produce powerful energy signatures that magnetize corresponding experiences. This is why the things we fear or try to avoid seem to arrive so effortlessly, while our deepest desires feel just out of reach.

The key, then, is not in efforting or striving, but in *unlearning*. It is in releasing what no longer serves, healing the inner distortions, and re-tuning our inner frequency to align with truth, abundance, and wholeness. This process requires a deliberate decision—to choose a new perception of reality, to reclaim our role as conscious creators, and to dissolve the illusion of separation from what we desire.

From a quantum perspective, reality is not fixed but fluid—a field of infinite potential that collapses into form through the act of observation. The observer effect in quantum mechanics illustrates that the act of observing something changes its behavior. In spiritual terms, this means that consciousness plays a central role in what becomes *real*. To manifest what we desire, we must become deliberate observers—choosing to see, feel, and embody that outcome as if it already exists.

In this light, the "realness" of our world does not lie in the objectivity of events, but in our decision to believe, perceive, and embody them. When we decide something is real—truly believe it in our hearts and align with it in our energy—it begins to materialize. Reality, then, is not something that happens *to* us, but something we allow, accept, and create.

Reflective Conclusion

The world you see is not fixed—it is a canvas awaiting the brushstroke of your awareness. Until you choose to declare something as real, it remains in the realm of potential, like unformed clay in the potter's hand. You are not merely a passive observer of your reality; you are its conscious architect. The power to shape your experience lies not in the outer world, but in your inner decision to believe, align, and embody the truth of what you desire.

So, ask yourself: *What are you choosing to believe is real today?*

Because reality is not waiting to reveal itself.

It's waiting for *you* to decide.

Chapter 6

Living a Magnetic and Extraordinary Life

Within me lies a glowing spark,
A force that lights both day and dark.
What I attract is what I feel,
My inner truth makes life more real.

No need to chase, no need to try,
I simply shine, and life draws nigh.
Aligned and whole, I rise above—
A life of grace, of power, and love.

The life we live is not random—it is the reflection of our energetic signature. Our inner state acts as a magnetic field, continuously attracting people, relationships, circumstances, and material experiences that resonate with the frequency we emit. In essence, we do not chase life; we magnetize it.

Yet, the challenge for many is that we remain disconnected from our true inner self. Conditioned by society, family, religion, and cultural systems, we often surrender our innate power to external authorities we deem more knowledgeable. Like sheep in a flock, we follow the guidance of others, blind to the shepherd within. In doing so, we silence the voice of our authentic self, burying it under layers of fear, guilt, and societal expectation.

Worse still, our inner fragmentation—shaped by personal wounds, generational trauma, and suppressed emotions—further distances us from wholeness. These soul fractures dilute our energetic integrity, making it harder to attract the life we deeply desire. But healing is possible. And in the process of reclaiming these lost fragments, we not only remember who we truly are—we return to sovereignty.

Individuals who walk the path of inner reclamation rediscover their inherent wholeness. With this wholeness comes power—a radiant magnetism born not from effort, but from alignment. They become masters of their own inner kingdom, no longer ruled by fear or dependency, but guided by clarity, freedom, and divine connection. They manifest from within, reflecting heaven on earth through a life that is both grounded and expansive.

To live a magnetic and extraordinary life is not about excess or perfection—it is about alignment, authenticity, and conscious intention. Philosophy offers timeless insights that can illuminate this path:

Philosophical Foundations of an Extraordinary Life

1. Embrace Authenticity (Existentialism)

Living authentically, as existentialists like Kierkegaard and Sartre propose, means aligning your actions with your core values. It's about shedding the masks we wear for societal approval and stepping into our truth—flawed, evolving, and real. This authenticity breeds inner peace and attracts genuine experiences.

2. Define and Pursue Purpose (Viktor Frankl)

Life's meaning isn't handed to us; we must define it. Frankl's work reminds us that purpose is a lifeline, even in suffering. When we align with purpose—by reflecting on our passions, setting meaningful goals, and contributing beyond ourselves—we fuel a life of depth and resilience.

3. Cultivate Resilience (Stoicism)

The Stoics taught that our power lies in how we respond, not in what happens. Building resilience through practices like mindfulness, gratitude, and self-inquiry strengthens our inner magnetism. We become grounded creators rather than reactive victims.

4. Connect with Nature (Transcendentalism)

Nature serves as a sacred mirror, reflecting simplicity, harmony, and wisdom. As Emerson and Thoreau showed, communion with nature reconnects us to the divine rhythm of life, quiets the noise, and awakens inspiration.

5. Celebrate the Ordinary (Mindful Living)

An extraordinary life is not only about grand accomplishments but also about finding beauty in the mundane. When we learn to be present and appreciative of simple joys, we experience richness and abundance in every moment.

6. Develop Charisma (Human Connection)

True charisma is magnetic. It's not a personality trait but a cultivated energy—through listening, presence, empathy, and sincere appreciation of others. When you shine from within, others feel it.

Reflective Conclusion

The Power of Inner Alignment

To live a magnetic and extraordinary life is not a privilege reserved for the few—it is a birthright accessible to all who dare to turn inward and reclaim their truth.

It begins with a choice: to stop outsourcing your power and to return home to yourself. It unfolds through courage—the courage to face your wounds, own your voice, and walk your unique path with integrity. And it expands as you realign with the energy of your soul, attracting a life that mirrors your deepest essence.

You are not here to live a muted, mechanical existence.

You are here to shine, to magnetize, to create, and to experience the extraordinary. The power is within you—*and always has been.*

Chapter 7

Need Nothing, Receive Everything

Let go the grasp, release the strain,
The sun still shines after the rain.
In wanting less, we come to see,
The heart grows full when it is free.

No chains of need, no heavy plea,
Just quiet trust in what will be.
In still surrender, we recall—
To need nothing… is to receive all.

Desire is an ever-present current in the human experience. It moves us, motivates us, and gives us a reason to strive. Much of what we do—working, planning, striving, creating—is driven by desire. But not all desires are the same. A subtle yet important distinction exists between a **need** and a **want.** While both spring from a sense of lack, they differ in urgency, essence, and emotional weight.

A **need** is considered essential—a requirement for survival, stability, or wellbeing. A **want**, on the other hand, is often a preference or craving—a desire for something that might enhance life but is not absolutely necessary. Yet in our fast-paced, consumption-driven culture, the line between needing and wanting has become increasingly blurred. We often chase wants as if they are needs, and in doing so, we fall into the trap of constant dissatisfaction.

As human beings, we are undeniably wired to ensure our basic needs are met—food, safety, connection, purpose. These fundamental drives push us to act, evolve, and adapt. But beyond these core necessities, we often become entangled in a web of ever-expanding desires—fueled by fear, comparison, insecurity, or the illusion of lack.

We are **powerful creators**, capable of shaping our reality with thoughts, intentions, and aligned actions. Yet many of us try to manifest from a place of **scarcity**—an inner belief that something is missing or broken. This lack-based mindset becomes the very barrier that blocks the flow of abundance. We desire outcomes but lack the **faith** and **patience** to wait for **Divine Timing**, attempting instead to control and force life according to our preferences.

Ironically, the more we grasp, the more we resist the very flow that brings things to us. In our yearning to feel emotionally secure *now*, we attempt to dictate how and when our desires should unfold. But the universe operates not by human will, but by divine orchestration. There is a greater intelligence that governs timing, alignment, and unfoldment—whether we acknowledge it or not.

When we surrender the illusion of control and **allow life to unfold**, we align with the rhythm of grace. This does not mean passivity or apathy—it means deep **trust**. It means choosing to believe that what is meant for us will never pass us by, and that what does arrive is not late nor early but perfectly timed.

Desires and attachments often create **resistance**. They impose conditions and timelines that block the free flow of blessings. When we say we "need" something to feel whole, we are subtly affirming that we are incomplete without it. That very belief can delay or distort manifestation. But when we release need and attachment—when we step into surrender—we discover an expansive truth: **everything we truly need is already within us or on its way to us.**

To **need nothing** is not to become cold or indifferent. It is to **anchor ourselves in the wholeness of the present moment.** It is a recognition that fulfillment is not about acquiring but about **receiving what is already here.** It is the quiet confidence that arises when we align with our higher self and trust that all is well—even if life doesn't look the way we expected.

This mindset shifts from **lack to abundance**, from **grasping to allowing**, is echoed in spiritual traditions around the world. In Buddhism, detachment from desire is a path to liberation. In mystical Christianity, surrender to Divine Will leads to grace and fulfillment. Across cultures and philosophies, the same message repeats: true abundance is not gained through accumulation, but through **alignment**.

Reflective Conclusion:

To "need nothing and receive everything" is not a passive resignation—it is the most powerful affirmation of **trust** in the divine order of life. It is a state of inner sufficiency, where we stop looking outside ourselves for validation, completion, or rescue. It is an invitation to rest in the stillness of the now, and to trust that the universe—when not obstructed by fear, doubt, or desperation—knows how to deliver what is meant for us.

In this sacred surrender, we open ourselves not only to the things we once desired—but to things far greater, far wiser, and far more aligned than what our limited minds could have imagined. We are no longer chasing. We are **receiving.**

Need nothing… and the universe gives you **everything.**

Chapter 8

The Soul's Curriculum: Lessons Hidden in Pain

In pain we break, in pain we bend,
Yet through the cracks, the light ascends.
A hidden path, a silent guide,
That leads us to the truth inside.

It strips away what isn't true,
Revealing depths, we never knew.
Not punishment, but love's disguise—
A gift that helps the soul arise.

Pain is an inevitable part of the human experience. It is not only a physical sensation triggered by injury or disease but also a deeply emotional and mental phenomenon shaped by our experiences, perceptions, and inner world. At its most basic biological level, pain serves as a crucial warning system—an intricate process involving nociceptors, the nervous system, and the brain. This system alerts us to potential harm and prompts us to take protective action, ensuring survival and initiating healing.

Yet pain extends beyond the physical body. Emotional and mental anguish—often triggered by loss, trauma, rejection, loneliness, or major life changes—can be just as, if not more, intense than physical pain. Chronic stress, unresolved conflicts, societal pressure, and mental health conditions like depression and anxiety add layers of complexity to our suffering. These experiences chip away at our sense of safety and stability, leading to feelings of hopelessness, worthlessness, and disconnection from self and others.

From a psychological standpoint, negative emotions and limited emotional awareness can worsen pain and hinder adaptation. Stressful life events, attachment insecurity, or unresolved trauma can increase emotional reactivity and deepen the impact of painful experiences. Over time, this emotional residue accumulates, leading to patterns of fear, avoidance, or numbness.

However, from a spiritual lens, pain is not just something to be endured—it is part of the soul's curriculum. It becomes a teacher, a compass, and a sacred initiator guiding us toward growth, transformation, and self-realization.

Pain as a Teacher

- **A Catalyst for Spiritual Awakening**
  Pain often becomes the force that pushes us inward. It strips away the superficial layers of life, demanding our full presence and attention. In moments of suffering, we are invited to explore deeper truths about ourselves and our existence.

- **A Mirror for the Soul's Needs**
  Pain reveals what is wounded, neglected, or misaligned within us. It points to unresolved grief, suppressed emotions, or unmet needs,

ultimately guiding us back to love, creativity, compassion, and authenticity.

- **A Gateway to Presence and Surrender**

  Suffering pulls us into the present moment, where past regrets and future anxieties fall away. It softens the ego's grip and beckons us to surrender—to trust something greater than our limited understanding.

- **An Invitation to Self-Inquiry**
  Pain compels us to ask difficult but necessary questions: Who am I? Why am I here? What truly matters? In seeking answers, we touch upon the deeper aspects of our identity and divine nature.

- **A Training Ground for Acceptance and Courage**

  By facing our pain rather than resisting it, we learn to transmute suffering into strength. Pain teaches us patience, resilience, and the courage to continue even when the path is uncertain or difficult.

Cultural and Philosophical Perspectives

- **Buddhism:** Suffering arises from attachment. Liberation comes through mindfulness, detachment, and cultivating compassion for all beings. Pain is a teacher that reveals the impermanence of life and the beauty of letting go.

- **Christianity:** Suffering is often seen as part of a divine plan, a means to strengthen faith and refine character. It is through trials that one learns endurance, deepens trust in God, and grows in Christlike love and humility.
- **Stoicism:** Pain is neutral; it is our judgment of pain that causes suffering. Stoics advocate for emotional regulation, accepting what we cannot control, and using adversity as a path to inner strength and peace.
- **Nietzsche:** "That which does not kill us makes us stronger." Suffering is not only inevitable but essential for personal growth, greatness, and the development of one's highest potential.

Key Takeaways

- Pain is both inevitable and essential—it holds within it the seeds of profound transformation.
- When approached with awareness, pain can initiate deep healing and spiritual growth.
- Practices such as meditation, prayer, breathwork, and authentic connection with others can help us process pain and extract wisdom from it.
- Suffering breaks down illusions, deepens empathy, and connects us with the universal human experience.

Reflective Conclusion

Pain is not the enemy of the soul—it is its greatest instructor. Hidden within suffering are sacred lessons that cannot be taught in comfort or ease. In pain, we meet the parts of ourselves we've avoided, denied, or abandoned. It strips us down to what is essential and reveals our truest essence.

When we shift from asking "Why is this happening to me?" to "What is this trying to teach me?", we begin to understand that pain is not punishment, but passage. It is a sacred initiation into a deeper awareness of who we are and who we are becoming.

The soul does not seek a life free from hardship. It seeks expansion, remembrance, and reunion with the Divine. And pain—raw, unwelcome, transformative pain—is often the crucible through which this remembering is made possible.

In surrendering to the lessons pain offers, we not only heal—we evolve. We awaken. We return to the light within, no longer fragmented by suffering but made whole by understanding.

Chapter 9

Coincidence: Not Random but Ordained

A stranger's smile, a timely word,
A dream repeated, gently stirred.
What chance could craft such perfect signs—
Unless by greater hand designed?

We call it luck, a twist, a nod,
But some see footprints left by God.
Not random steps, but paths aligned—
A secret order, soul refined.

Coincidences are events or circumstances that appear related but lack a clear causal connection. They often feel remarkable or surprising, seemingly defying the odds. While some dismiss them as mere chance, others perceive them as meaningful signs—possibly even spiritual messages.

Psychologists often explain coincidences through *cognitive biases*, particularly *confirmation bias*—our tendency to seek or interpret information that aligns with our preexisting beliefs. This unconscious filtering causes us to notice and remember coincidences that seem to validate our personal narratives, while disregarding those that don't. From a statistical standpoint, the sheer volume of daily events makes some degree of coincidence inevitable. What seems improbable on the surface becomes more likely when viewed through the lens of vast possibilities.

Yet not all coincidences can be easily explained by logic or probability. Some occurrences defy simple causation and strike us with a sense of mystery, depth, or timing too precise to be accidental.

This is where the concept of *synchronicity*, introduced by Carl Jung, emerges. Synchronicity refers to "meaningful coincidences"—events that may not have a direct cause-and-effect link but hold deep, personal significance for the individual experiencing them. Unlike coincidences, which are often viewed as random or meaningless, synchronicities feel guided, purposeful, and symbolically rich. They transcend mere probability, resonating with our inner world in ways that suggest a higher order at play.

The key distinction lies in interpretation:

- **Coincidence** is often perceived as objective and random.
- **Synchronicity** is experienced as subjectively meaningful and spiritually potent.

From a spiritual and metaphysical perspective, many traditions hold that coincidences—especially those that evoke strong emotional or intuitive responses—are *not random*, but rather *ordained*. They are viewed as signs, guidance, or messages orchestrated by a higher power. In this view, nothing happens by accident; every encounter, detour, or "chance" meeting is part of a divine blueprint.

Even science, particularly quantum physics, adds nuance to the conversation. Quantum entanglement, a phenomenon in which two particles remain interconnected regardless of distance, challenges traditional notions of time and causality. When one particle is measured, the other responds instantly—what Einstein famously called "spooky action at a distance." This suggests a reality in which non-local connections are possible, echoing the interconnectedness implied in spiritual interpretations of coincidence.

The belief that "coincidence is not random but ordained" is echoed in religious doctrines such as Divine Providence, where God is believed to orchestrate all things to fulfill a greater plan. Scriptures offer examples—from Ruth choosing a particular field to the apostles casting lots—where events that appear coincidental are later revealed to be pivotal moments in a larger divine narrative.

Ultimately, whether through the lens of spirituality, psychology, or quantum mechanics, the idea persists that life may be more ordered and meaningful than it first appears. What we label as "coincidence" may in fact be the universe whispering—softly, precisely, and intentionally—guiding us along a path only later revealed in full.

Reflective Conclusion

To see coincidences not as random but as *ordained* requires a shift in perception—from randomness to reverence. It invites us to consider the possibility that our lives are interwoven with a deeper intelligence, one that speaks not in certainty, but in symbols and synchronicities. In choosing to see with spiritual eyes, we open ourselves to wonder, humility, and a profound trust that we are being gently led, even when we do not understand the way.

Chapter 10

You Are Not Your Thoughts

Thoughts may rise like ocean tides,
Whispers soft or roaring wide.
But you, dear soul, are not their voice—
You hold the power; you have the choice.

They come and go like clouds above,
Yet you remain, pure light and love.
So, watch them drift, both dark and bright—
You are the stillness, not the fight.

As human beings, we are gifted with a highly evolved brain. With this gift comes the capacity for complex cognition: the ability to reason, process information, and form abstract ideas. These capabilities not only serve our survival but also grant us the power to transcend limitations and create realities shaped by the mind. Because of this, it is easy—almost automatic—to identify ourselves with our thoughts.

What Are Thoughts?

Thoughts are mental processes that encompass a wide range of activities: reasoning, remembering, imagining, problem-solving, and interpreting the world. They shape our beliefs, opinions, and perceptions—essentially forming the lens through which we understand and interact with life. Thoughts can be:

- **Conscious**, such as planning your day or recalling a memory.
- **Unconscious**, influencing behavior without our awareness.
- **Verbal**, expressed in internal dialogue or self-talk.
- **Non-verbal**, experienced as images, sensations, or emotions.

Types of thoughts include:

- **Conceptual thoughts:** Ideas, values, or beliefs about ourselves and the world.
- **Perceptual thoughts:** Derived from sensory experiences (e.g., seeing, hearing, tasting).
- **Emotional thoughts:** Tied to feelings such as joy, anger, fear, or sadness.
- **Problem-solving thoughts:** Focused on decision-making and strategizing.

These thoughts are part of a broader system of cognition, involving perception, attention, memory, language, and reasoning. They help us make meaning of the world, integrating past experiences and learned knowledge into a coherent mental landscape.

The Overload of Thought

Studies suggest that humans process thousands of thoughts per day—estimates range from 6,000 to over 70,000. Much of this activity is automatic or unconscious. Given the sheer volume, it's easy to get lost in this inner stream and equate our identity with the noise of the mind.

We might say, *"I am anxious," "I am not good enough,"* or *"I can't do this,"* forgetting that these are simply thoughts—not truths. When we over-identify with these mental narratives, they begin to shape our emotional states, behavior, and even the reality we create for ourselves.

Spiritual Perspective: You Are the Awareness Behind the Thoughts

From a spiritual or mindfulness-based viewpoint, the statement *"You are not your thoughts"* means that your true essence lies not in the thoughts themselves but in the awareness that observes them. This awareness is steady and unchanging, while thoughts are fleeting and ever-shifting—much like clouds drifting across the sky or waves forming and dissolving on the surface of the ocean.

Key Insights from This Perspective:

- **Thoughts as Events**: Thoughts are passing phenomena. Just as weather doesn't define the sky, our thoughts don't define who we are.
- **Awareness as Observer**: Our true self is the silent witness—the consciousness in which thoughts arise and fall.

- **Disidentification:** Recognizing that we are not our thoughts allows us to observe them with detachment. We gain the freedom to respond rather than react, cultivating emotional clarity and mental peace.
- **Influence of Thought:** While we are not defined by our thoughts, they influence our perceptions, actions, and reality. Thus, mindful thinking supports a more empowered and liberated experience of life.

Reflective Conclusion: The Power of Inner Distance

In a world saturated with mental noise, remembering that *you are not your thoughts* is both a profound truth and a liberating practice. You are not your worries, your regrets, your self-criticisms, or even your ambitions. You are the one who sees them.

This awareness is the seat of your power. By learning to witness your thoughts without attaching your identity to them, you become free from mental entanglement. This freedom is not passive—it is transformative. It opens the door to conscious living, allowing you to respond with wisdom, rather than react from habit.

So, the next time a thought arises—whether joyful or fearful—pause, take a breath, and remember:
You are the sky, not the passing clouds.
You are the awareness, not the mind's chatter.
You are not your thoughts. You are something far deeper—vast, luminous, and free.

Chapter 11

Alchemy Through Quantum Principles

In fields unseen, we plant a thought,
A spark of light, a dream long sought.
With heart aligned and soul made clear,
The universe begins to steer.

No wish too small, no step too slow,
In quantum winds, the currents flow.
Believe, intend, and gently see—
You shape the world through what you be

Quantum physics is the language of the unseen, the framework of the subatomic world where reality behaves in mysterious and counterintuitive ways. At the heart of this field lie four core principles: **wave-particle duality**, **superposition**, **entanglement**, and the **uncertainty principle**. Together, these describe how energy and matter interact in ways that transcend classical physics—and possibly point to deeper truths about our own consciousness and creative power.

Core Quantum Principles

- **Wave-Particle Duality:**

  Quantum entities such as electrons display both wave-like and particle-like behavior. Depending on how they are observed, they can behave like particles with mass and momentum, or like waves capable of interference and diffraction. This duality challenges the traditional notion of fixed identity in matter.

- **Superposition:**
  A quantum system can exist in multiple states simultaneously until it is observed or measured. This principle, illustrated by Schrödinger's cat thought experiment, suggests that reality holds a range of potential outcomes—all coexisting in possibility until one is actualized.

- **Entanglement:**
  Entangled particles share a deep connection, such that the state of one instantly influences the state of another, regardless of distance. This phenomenon points to a universe where everything is interconnected beyond space and time.

- **Uncertainty Principle (Heisenberg):**
  This principle states that we cannot precisely know both the position and momentum of a particle at the same time. The more accurately we measure one, the less we know about the other—suggesting a fundamental fuzziness at the core of existence.

Quantum Principles and Manifestation

Beyond their scientific value, these quantum ideas inspire philosophical and metaphysical perspectives—especially regarding human consciousness and the power to influence reality. The emerging concept of **quantum manifestation** posits that by aligning thought, emotion, and intention, one can interact with the quantum field to co-create outcomes in life.

1. Entanglement and Interconnectedness

Just as particles become entangled, our thoughts and emotions may interact with the quantum field. It is believed that when we focus with clarity on a desire, we energetically link ourselves to that possibility, drawing it closer into our experience.

2. The Observer Effect and Shaping Reality

The observer effect shows that observation alters quantum behavior. In the realm of manifestation, this translates into the idea that **conscious focus shapes outcome**. What we give attention to begins to collapse into form.

3. Energy, Frequency, and Emotional Alignment

Everything in the quantum world vibrates with energy. Emotions such as love, gratitude, and joy emit higher frequencies. By cultivating these states, we align ourselves with the energy of the realities we wish to attract.

4. Intention as Catalyst

Just as an electron responds to intention through observation, so too may our intentions act as triggers for synchronicities and change. Strong, clear intentions can be the energetic spark that initiates a chain of unfolding events.

5. Belief and Perception

In quantum terms, **perception affects reality**. The same holds true in life—what we believe becomes the lens through which our reality forms. A shift in belief can lead to a profound shift in experience.

Practical Applications of Quantum-Inspired Manifestation

- Set clear and emotionally charged intentions.
- Practice gratitude and cultivate elevated emotions to shift your vibratory frequency.
- Visualize your desired reality with focus and consistency.
- Align your actions with your vision—manifestation requires effort, not just wishful thinking.
- Release limiting beliefs and unresolved trauma that may block your energy.
- Trust in the unfolding of the universe without clinging to outcomes.

Important Considerations

While quantum principles offer profound insights, caution is warranted in applying them too literally to manifestation or metaphysical claims. Many physicists emphasize that these ideas are often misinterpreted when taken outside their scientific context. However, whether symbolic or literal, these principles offer powerful metaphors for personal transformation and empowerment.

The heart of quantum alchemy is not about bypassing effort or expecting miracles overnight. Rather, it is about understanding the invisible patterns that shape our experience—and learning to dance with them consciously.

Reflective Conclusion

The wisdom of quantum physics teaches us that reality is not a rigid structure, but a field of infinite possibilities. We are not mere observers—we are participatory creators. Each thought, emotion, and intention ripples across the field of potentiality, influencing what collapses into form.

When we attune our inner world to clarity, alignment, and elevated emotion, we become living alchemists—shaping matter with the unseen tools of mind and spirit. This is the sacred bridge where science meets mysticism, and where knowledge becomes power.

The quantum field is not just "out there"—it is within us. And in learning its language, we rediscover our innate power to co-create not only our reality but a higher version of ourselves.

Chapter 12

Alpha State: Gateway Through the Subconscious

In stillness soft, the mind lets go,
Where silent streams of insight flow.
Between the thoughts, a gentle hum,
The door to deeper truths becomes.

Not fully wake, not yet in sleep,
The soul begins its climb so deep.
A sacred space, so calm, so wide—
Where dreams and wisdom both reside.

In the vast and intricate workings of the human brain lies a remarkable rhythm—an electrical symphony composed of oscillating waves, each operating at different frequencies. These brainwaves are typically measured in Hertz (Hz), reflecting the number of cycles per second. From the rapid activity of beta waves to the deep, slow rhythms of delta, these frequencies govern our states of consciousness, shaping how we think, feel, perceive, and even heal.

Among these, the **alpha brainwave state**—ranging between 7.5 to 14 Hz—holds a unique and powerful position. It is often described as a **gateway to the subconscious mind**, a bridge between our alert, logical thoughts and the vast, symbolic realm beneath them. Unlike the high-frequency beta waves

(14–30 Hz) that dominate our waking life—those responsible for active thinking, problem-solving, and alertness—the alpha state emerges when we slow down, relax, and become inwardly still. It typically surfaces when we close our eyes, take deep breaths, or engage in peaceful activities like daydreaming, creative visualization, or light meditation.

This state of relaxed awareness fosters a **heightened receptivity,** a moment where the conscious mind gently steps aside and allows access to the deeper layers of self. Here, in the subtle hum of alpha frequencies, we begin to quiet the internal noise and open the door to intuitive wisdom, creativity, and insight. Artists, musicians, inventors, and mystics have long tapped into this state, sometimes unknowingly, during moments of inspiration and flow. It is in the alpha state that we are most attuned to flashes of creativity, problem-solving "aha!" moments, and spontaneous realizations that seem to arise out of nowhere.

Neuroscience supports what ancient meditative traditions have known for centuries: the alpha state plays a critical role in **learning, memory consolidation, and emotional regulation.** When the brain enters this state, it becomes more plastic—more open to absorbing new information and restructuring old patterns. For this reason, alpha frequencies are often harnessed in **hypnotherapy**, **guided meditation**, and **affirmation practices** to plant new beliefs, overwrite limiting thought patterns, and promote healing.

Moreover, this state is associated with **lower levels of cortisol**, the stress hormone, which explains why people often feel more relaxed, centered, and balanced after engaging in alpha-inducing practices. From a therapeutic standpoint, this makes the alpha state an ideal platform for initiating **subconscious healing and transformation.**

Techniques for entering the alpha state are accessible and varied. **Mindfulness meditation**, **deep diaphragmatic breathing**, **visualization exercises**, and **progressive muscle relaxation** are among the most effective. Even simple practices—like gazing at a candle flame, listening to ambient music, watching waves roll onto a beach, or walking quietly in nature—can gently guide the brain into alpha rhythms. In essence, any activity that quiets the mind and softens the internal dialogue invites alpha frequencies to arise.

What makes the alpha state particularly compelling is its role as a **liminal space**—a threshold between the outer world of physical reality and the inner world of intuitive knowing. It is in this threshold that we gain access to repressed memories, core beliefs, emotional imprints, and inner archetypes. It is also where we can rewrite our inner narrative, update our subconscious programming, and align more deeply with the truth of who we are. When accessed consistently, the alpha state becomes a **portal to self-mastery**.

In modern life, however, the pace of the world often keeps us locked in beta wave dominance—constant stimulation, multitasking, stress, and information overload. This chronic overactivation can distance us from the subtle and healing properties of the alpha state. When we forget to slow down and become present, we inadvertently block the very access point to inner peace, intuitive insight, and subconscious realignment.

Thus, the invitation becomes clear: to regularly return to stillness, to intentionally create space for relaxation, and to allow the alpha state to become part of our daily rhythm. When we do so, we not only sharpen our mental faculties and emotional balance but also rekindle our connection to the **subconscious wellspring of wisdom** that resides within each of us.

Reflective Conclusion

The alpha state is more than just a neural frequency—it is a **sacred bridge** between thought and knowing, doing and being, noise and silence. In this space, the mind quiets, the heart softens, and the soul begins to speak. To access this state is to remember the power of stillness and the intelligence of the subconscious.

When we learn to honor the alpha rhythm, we reclaim an inner sanctuary where clarity replaces confusion, creativity flows effortlessly, and healing becomes possible. It is here—between the seen and unseen, the conscious and the subconscious—that we begin to truly *know ourselves*. And in that knowing, transformation unfolds.

Chapter 13

Our Purpose is Our Function

A spark within, a quiet call,
A reason why we rise at all.
Not always loud, not always clear,
Yet purpose whispers, "You belong here."

It's not in fame or fortune's gleam,
But in each act, each simple dream.
To heal, to help, to plant, to mend,
In every start, in every end.

So, walk your path, both slow and true,
The world is better just for you.

What is the value of life itself without purpose? This is the deepest existential question every soul eventually asks. The moment consciousness awakens within the confines of physical form, there begins a longing—a yearning to understand *why* it chose to incarnate in this specific time, space, and set of circumstances. Purpose is more than a goal; it is the very reason for our existence. It becomes the soul's compass, pointing the way through the ever-changing currents of life.

Purpose fuels the spirit. It energizes our journey and anchors us in meaning when everything else feels uncertain. While we often search for answers to "what" and "where," it is the question of *why* that propels us forward. The "why" sustains us when the path becomes difficult. It gives life shape, meaning, and direction.

When we align with our purpose, we come alive. It shapes our identity in this particular timeline. Purpose becomes more than just an abstract idea—it becomes *function.* Like a tool designed for a specific task, we too carry an inherent design. Our talents, tendencies, and passions are not random. They point toward what we are uniquely meant to do. Just as a chair finds fulfillment in supporting weight, we fulfill our essence when we step into our function.

But purpose is not just about external accomplishments or roles. It is both *inner* and *outer.* The outer purpose may change with seasons—career paths, relationships, creative pursuits—but the inner purpose often remains the same: to be present, to love, to grow in awareness, to serve, to create. Inner purpose is about being, while outer purpose is about doing. When both are aligned, a deep sense of harmony emerges.

Some believe that purpose is divinely prewritten, a sacred design etched into the blueprint of our soul. Others believe it is crafted and shaped by our free will and evolving self-awareness. In truth, it may be both. We are given seeds of purpose, but it is through choice, experience, and inner work that we cultivate those seeds into something meaningful.

Importantly, purpose doesn't have to be grand or universally recognized. It need not be tied to fame, fortune, or praise. Purpose is deeply personal. If planting a garden, rescuing animals, making people laugh, or bringing kindness to strangers brings joy to your heart, then that is your sacred function. What matters is *how* it makes you feel—and *how* it connects you to the world.

Sometimes, not knowing our purpose initially is a blessing in disguise. It gives us the opportunity to explore, to fail, to create, and to rediscover ourselves. In that process, we learn that we are not victims of fate, but co-creators of our destiny. We can choose, refine, or even redefine our purpose as we evolve. And that fluidity is powerful.

Knowing your purpose reminds you that you *matter*. It gives meaning to your actions, clarity to your choices, and strength to your spirit. It helps you tap into the best version of yourself and deepens your sense of connection—to others, to the world, and to something greater than you. And in that connection, fear of the unknown begins to dissolve.

Reflective Conclusion

Purpose is the soul's compass. It guides, aligns, and illuminates the path ahead. Whether discovered through divine revelation or creative exploration, purpose transforms life from a series of random events into a meaningful journey. When we live according to our purpose—however big or small it may seem—we step into a fuller version of ourselves. We contribute, we grow, and we shine. And in doing so, we come to realize that our presence in this world is not accidental. It is essential.

So, whatever your path may look like—be it a whisper or a roar—know that your purpose is your gift to the world. Find it. Live it. Be it.

Chapter 14

Surrender: Trusting the Wisdom of the Unknown

Let go the grip, release the fight,
Not all is seen in morning light.
The path unfolds when we are still,
Not through the force, but through the will.

Trust the dark where stars are sown,
There lies the wisdom of the Unknown.
In letting go, we come to see—
What's meant to be will always be.

Technically, to *surrender* means to cease resistance to an enemy or opponent and submit to their authority. In the realm of spirituality, however, this concept takes on a more profound meaning. Here, surrender is not about defeat but about yielding to a higher intelligence, a divine order, or circumstances ordained by a source greater than us.

Surrender, in this deeper sense, is not an easy feat. We are conditioned by the primal survival responses of *fight or flight*—mechanisms deeply embedded in the human psyche. These instincts compel us to resist, to fight back, to assert control at all costs. Only when we've exhausted every resource, when resistance becomes unsustainable or counterproductive, do we consider surrender—as a last resort, a reluctant strategy to preserve something precious or avoid greater loss.

But there's another kind of surrender—one far more subtle and spiritually transformative: *the surrender to the unknown.* Unlike surrendering to a known adversary or force, this type involves relinquishing control to something we cannot fully perceive or predict. It is the willingness to trust in what we do not yet understand.

We are beings constantly projecting ourselves into the future. We worry about what lies ahead because we are uncomfortable with not knowing. We crave clarity and certainty, demanding answers *now*, unwilling to wait for life to unfold in its natural rhythm. Our impatience is fueled by fear—the fear of loss, failure, or being caught off guard. And in this fear-driven state, we strive to control outcomes, believing that mastery over circumstances will offer peace.

Yet, life often works in paradoxes. The more we try to control it, the more elusive it becomes—almost as if it slips through our fingers intentionally, reminding us that control is often an illusion.

To surrender to the wisdom of the unknown is to consciously release this illusion. It is to let go of the compulsive need to micromanage life and to place trust in a higher order—whether you call it God, the Universe, the Divine, or simply life itself. It's an invitation to embrace uncertainty not as a threat but as a space of infinite possibility.

This form of surrender is not about passivity or resignation. On the contrary, it requires tremendous courage. It is an act of inner strength to admit that we don't have all the answers and to be at peace with that. It is about taking inspired action when needed but letting go of attachment to outcomes. It is trusting that even if things do not go according to plan, there is still a greater plan unfolding—one that serves our highest growth.

Surrender, then, is the gateway to inner peace. It is the quiet confidence that arises when we stop resisting life and instead move in harmony with its current. It allows us to let go of fear, open ourselves to new possibilities, and deepen our connection to the sacred intelligence that animates all of existence.

Reflective Conclusion

Surrendering to the unknown is not an admission of weakness—it is an act of radical trust. It is choosing faith over fear, flow over force, and acceptance over anxiety. In a world that glorifies control, surrender calls us back to a deeper truth: that life is not a problem to be solved, but a mystery to be lived.

To surrender is to remember that we are not alone in this journey. There is wisdom woven into the chaos, meaning hidden within uncertainty, and guidance available when we are still enough to listen. The unknown is not our enemy—it is the fertile soil of transformation. And when we learn to trust it, we don't lose our power—we reclaim our peace.

Chapter 15

True Power Lies Not in Control but in Surrender

We seek to grasp, to hold, to steer,
To tame the winds, to calm the fear.
But life flows wild, not made to bind—
It teaches peace in heart and mind.

True strength is not in tight control,
But in surrender of the soul.
To trust the path, though dim or wide,
And let the deeper truth decide.

So, breathe, release, and gently flow,
Let life unfold, just let it grow.
In yielding soft, the strong are known—
For those who bend, will not be thrown.

There are too many moving parts in our existence that lie far beyond our capacity to control. These are mostly external forces—volatile, unpredictable, and influenced by countless variables we can neither anticipate nor comprehend. What we can truly control, however, is our inner world—how we respond to circumstances, how we process our emotions, and how we choose to act amidst uncertainty. Even this form of mastery requires effort, self-awareness, maturity, and a refined mindset.

As human beings, the impulse to control is deeply embedded in our psyche. And understandably so—control gives us a sense of power, of safety, of order in an otherwise chaotic world. We feel happy, secure, and validated when we believe things are going our way. Yet life has a way of unraveling even the most carefully constructed plans. Accidents occur, relationships shift, health falters, and events unfold in ways we never imagined. When these happen, we panic, grasp tighter, and paradoxically, the more we try to control, the more chaos we create.

These disruptions force us to question the very foundation of our belief in control. Are we ever truly in command, or is this just a comforting illusion that helps us feel powerful in an unpredictable world? In moments of helplessness, we often fall into victimhood—believing that we are at the mercy of a higher power or fate, subject to forces beyond our understanding.

If we perceive these higher forces as distant, indifferent, or even malevolent—as often portrayed in traditional religious texts—our sense of disempowerment deepens. For example, the Old Testament recounts how Adam and Eve were cast out of Eden for disobedience, or how Abraham was tested by being asked to sacrifice his beloved son, Isaac. Such stories reflect a dynamic where God appears controlling, punitive, and arbitrary.

But mystical traditions offer a radically different view. In these perspectives, we are not separate from the Creator—we are individualized expressions of that same divine essence. This creative force, often called Source or the Divine, chose to experience itself through form, through limitation, and through the trials of human existence. In this framework, our lives are not isolated events, but carefully orchestrated experiences designed for growth, expansion, and remembrance of our true nature.

If we embrace this view, we begin to see life not as something happening *to* us, but *through* us. The dance between the higher and lower aspects of ourselves becomes a sacred co-creation—each challenge an invitation to expand, each moment of surrender a return to truth.

From this understanding, we arrive at a powerful paradox: **True power lies not in control, but in surrender.** Surrender does not mean giving up or being passive. Rather, it means letting go of the illusion that we must (or can) control everything. It means aligning ourselves with the natural rhythm of life and trusting in a higher intelligence that guides our unfolding.

Letting go of control can feel counterintuitive, especially in a world that glorifies dominance, certainty, and perfection. But surrender opens us to deeper awareness, inner peace, and greater flexibility. It allows us to redirect our energy from resisting what is, to flowing with it.

Surrender acknowledges our limitations with humility and grace. It invites presence, authenticity, and inner strength. When we release the need to manipulate how others perceive us or how life should unfold, we become more genuine. This authenticity deepens our relationships, enhances creativity, and brings a quiet confidence that cannot be shaken by external circumstances.

In relationships, surrender means releasing the need to change or control others. It cultivates compassion, respect, and mutual growth. In professional life, it means empowering others rather than micromanaging, creating space for collaboration and innovation. In personal development, surrendering to the process of growth—even with all its imperfections—opens the door to true self-acceptance and fulfillment.

Spiritual traditions across cultures emphasize surrender as a path to enlightenment and union with the divine. Whether it's through prayer, meditation, mindfulness, or stillness, surrender reconnects us to a higher intelligence within and around us—one that holds a wisdom far greater than our limited perspective.

Reflective Conclusion

The Power of Surrender

To surrender is not to lose, but to awaken. It is not weakness, but a profound act of inner strength. In surrender, we acknowledge that while we are not in control of all things, we are participants in a much grander unfolding—a divine orchestration that seeks to evolve, refine, and elevate our consciousness.

When we stop striving to dominate life and instead allow life to flow through us, we tap into a deeper source of power—one rooted in trust, presence, and peace. True power is not about bending life to our will but about bending with life in wisdom.

In surrender, we find resilience.

In surrender, we find grace.

And in surrender, we finally come home to the deeper truth of who we are.

Chapter 16

Destiny: Not a Fixed Outcome but a Frequency

Not set in stone, nor carved by fate,
But shaped by love we cultivate.
A song we sing with every choice,
In every thought, a silent voice.

It's not a place we're meant to find,
But a rhythm flowing through the mind.
Align your heart, your truth, your way—
And destiny will start to play.

Destiny is traditionally defined as a predetermined course of events, often perceived to be orchestrated by a divine force or governed by an immutable cosmic plan. People often refer to destiny when reflecting on life-altering events that feel fated—"It was their destiny to meet," or "He believed it was his destiny to become a great leader." These statements suggest an inevitability, as if life is a script already written, where our role is merely to act out what has already been decided. Under this paradigm, regardless of the choices we make or the paths we take, the final outcome remains unchanged—a fixed destination beyond our power to influence or rewrite.

But such a belief can subtly disempower. It implies that we are passengers in our own journey, not co-creators of our fate. It places our sense of purpose at the mercy of forces beyond our control, suggesting that life is about arriving at a specific endpoint—an ordained event, title, or status—instead of exploring the unfolding richness of the path itself.

Philosophically, however, a deeper truth emerges what truly matters is not the destination, but the journey. It is through the twists and turns, the heartbreaks and triumphs, that the soul evolves. In every hero's quest, the protagonist begins as innocent and naive, unaware of their inner strength or higher calling. Through trials and challenges, they are transformed—not merely by reaching a final goal, but by *becoming* something greater in the process. This metamorphosis is the real gold, far more valuable than any material reward or title achieved at the end.

From this lens, destiny is not a rigid outcome etched in stone, but a living, breathing potential—a *frequency* the soul attunes to over time. It is fluid, evolutionary, and responsive to the vibrational state of our being. Destiny, then, is not something waiting for us at the end of a straight path, but something we *generate* and *shape* through our choices, intentions, emotions, and the resonance of our energy.

Much like an alchemist turning base metals into gold, the soul undergoes its own alchemy—refining, purifying, and elevating itself through experience. This spiritual transformation requires a shift from the dense vibration of fixed beliefs and ego attachments to the expansive frequency of conscious awareness and alignment. In this way, destiny becomes a dynamic flow, a dance of frequency that reflects our internal state and spiritual readiness.

Quantum mechanics offers a metaphor for this idea. In the quantum field, particles do not have fixed locations until observed—they exist in a state of probability, a wave of potential outcomes. In the same way, our lives are not carved in linear stone but ripple with countless possibilities that shift with our conscious focus. Every thought, emotion, and intention emit a vibrational signature that interacts with the field of reality, drawing experiences that match our frequency.

When we consciously choose empowering thoughts, nourish loving emotions, and act with integrity and clarity, we elevate our vibration. This elevation aligns us with more expansive and fulfilling timelines—what might be called our "highest destiny." We become magnetic to opportunities, relationships, and synchronicities that match our energetic resonance.

This perspective reframes destiny from a passive endpoint into an *active creation.* It reminds us that we are not victims of fate, but co-creators with the universe. Rather than asking, "What is my destiny?" we begin to ask, "What frequency am I holding—and what future is it calling in?"

Reflective Conclusion

Destiny, in its truest form, is not a destination stamped in the stars—it is the soul's harmonic alignment with its highest truth. It is not fixed, but flexible. Not static, but fluid. Like music, it flows in vibrations, shaped by the chords we strike within ourselves. The more conscious we become of our internal state—our thoughts, emotions, and intentions—the more deliberate we become in tuning into the frequency of our desired future.

We are not here merely to reach an end. We are here to *remember*, to *transform*, and to *create*. In each moment, we are sculpting our path—not by force, but by frequency. And when we align with love, clarity, purpose, and truth, destiny is not something we chase—it is something we naturally attract.

So, ask not what your destiny is. Ask instead:

What am I vibrating today?

And let your destiny rise to meet you there

Chapter 17

Boundaries: Sacred Spaces of the Soul

A quiet space within the soul,
Where only truth is in control.
Not walls that shut the world away,
But light that guides us through the day.

A gentle "yes," a mindful "no,"
To guard the peace and let love grow.
In knowing self, we stand so free—
Aligned in strength and clarity.

We constantly exchange energy through our interactions—with people, places, and even thoughts. Yet, many of us move through life unaware of how these exchanges affect us on a subtle, energetic level. Each person carries emotional baggage, and every thought holds a unique vibrational imprint. These vibrations influence how we think, how we feel, and ultimately, how we experience reality.

Our vibrational state is not fixed; it can shift moment by moment depending on our focus and awareness. When we entertain fear-based thoughts, we immediately slip into survival mode—fight, flight, or freeze—as a means of self-preservation. Conversely, when we focus on love, unity, and trust, we expand, radiate compassion, and view life through a more harmonious lens. This constant fluctuation between contraction and expansion presents the soul with a fundamental challenge: *the choice of alignment.*

At the heart of this challenge lies our most profound gift—**free will.** Free will is the power to choose our state of being, to consciously decide where we place our attention, and how we respond to life's stimuli. But free will should be used judiciously—not impulsively. True freedom comes not from reacting unconsciously, but from responding with awareness. Unfortunately, most of our decisions are reactionary, rooted in subconscious programming rather than mindful discernment.

Why do we react instead of respond? One significant reason is the inability to distinguish between what energy belongs to us and what comes from others. When we absorb external energies without discernment—be it through relationships, environments, or collective fears—we become energetically entangled. Add to this the deep, often unhealed layers of generational and collective trauma, and the result is confusion, misjudgment, and repeated suffering.

We live amid a complex vibrational ecosystem—a constant energetic crossfire. To preserve clarity and integrity, we must *maintain our own energy field.* This is where the importance of boundaries becomes clear.

Boundaries are not barriers. They are *sacred spaces*—intentional zones that protect our emotional, spiritual, and energetic sovereignty. When we speak of boundaries as sacred, we acknowledge their role in nurturing the soul's evolution. These are not rigid walls but porous, living membranes—capable of discernment, able to welcome in love and connection, and simultaneously filter out noise, toxicity, and distraction.

Creating and maintaining boundaries allows us to remain aligned with our divine purpose, rather than being swept away by every emotional current or interpersonal drama. Setting boundaries is not selfish—it is a conscious act of devotion to one's own well-being. It means choosing wisely rather than reacting blindly. It means honoring your path while allowing others to walk theirs without overstepping or losing yourself.

Boundaries provide internal space for *clarity, rest, reflection, and rejuvenation.* They are islands of consciousness where the soul can replenish its light, listen to its inner voice, and make choices rooted in truth. From this space of centeredness, we can engage with the world from a place of integrity rather than fragmentation.

To set boundaries is to say:

"I know who I am. I honor my energy. I respect my journey."

Reflective Conclusion

Boundaries are not limits—they are invitations to wholeness. They help us navigate life with clarity, protecting our essence while guiding us toward alignment with our higher selves. In a world where energy is constantly moving and merging, sacred boundaries serve as soul-defined thresholds—allowing us to live authentically, love wisely, and choose consciously.

In honoring our sacred spaces, we do not isolate ourselves—we simply return to ourselves. And from that place of inner safety, we meet the world with open hearts and anchored presence.

Chapter 18

The Glass Is Neither Half Full nor Half Empty—It Simply Is

Not half full,
Not half gone,
The glass stands still,
Just moving on.

No need to weigh
What's less or more—
Life flows in truth,
No need to score.

Be here, be now,
Let labels cease.
In what just is,
We find our peace.

We often describe people as either optimists or pessimists based on how they interpret the classic metaphor of the glass: half full or half empty. Optimists are celebrated for seeing the bright side, for being hopeful and confident in the future. Pessimists, on the other hand, are often criticized for their tendency to focus on what's lacking or what could go wrong. Society frequently promotes optimism as the superior trait, reinforcing its psychological and physiological benefits.

However, this binary view overlooks a more grounded and often wiser approach: realism.

The Case for Optimism

Optimism is associated with numerous benefits. Optimists tend to have better mental health, higher levels of happiness, and greater resilience. They cope better with stress, enjoy stronger immune function, and may even live longer. Optimism fuels motivation, supports creative thinking, and helps individuals bounce back after failures. It encourages a belief that good ultimately triumphs over evil—a hopeful stance that can energize people in the face of adversity.

The Pitfalls of Excessive Optimism

Yet, unchecked optimism has its drawbacks. It can lead to unrealistic expectations, poor decision-making, and vulnerability to disappointment. When optimism clouds judgment, people may ignore risks, misread warning signs, or overestimate their abilities. Overconfidence born from constant positivity can lead to failure, not because of lack of effort, but because of lack of preparation.

Understanding Pessimism

Pessimism, although often viewed negatively, also has a psychological role. Pessimists tend to be more cautious, risk-averse, and aware of potential pitfalls. This mindset can act as a safeguard against reckless behavior. However, persistent pessimism can breed chronic negativity, depression, and hopelessness. It can hinder personal growth, dampen relationships, and contribute to poorer health outcomes.

The Need for Balance

Rather than promoting one perspective over another, it's essential to recognize the strengths and weaknesses of both. A healthy mindset may not lie solely in optimism or pessimism, but in finding a balance—what psychologists might call "realistic optimism." This approach embraces the hopeful spirit of optimism while remaining grounded in practicality and truth. It allows for adaptability, sound decision-making, and emotional stability, particularly when facing uncertainty.

The Realist Perspective: Seeing Things as They Are

Beyond optimism and pessimism lies realism—a viewpoint that neither exaggerates the good nor fixates on the bad. Realists seek to understand life as it is. They do not view the glass as half full or half empty; they simply acknowledge the glass contains water, and that's what matters.

Realism invites us to engage with the present moment without the distortions of excessive hope or fear. It encourages acceptance—of what is, rather than what could or should be. Realists value facts over feelings, presence over projection, and practicality over fantasy. They take action based on reality, not illusion, and in doing so, cultivate inner peace and external effectiveness.

Reflective Conclusion

Embracing Life as It Is

In a world often obsessed with labeling perspectives as positive or negative, the wisdom of realism reminds us that life is best lived in the now, as it unfolds. When we step away from the need to categorize our experience—half full or half empty—we begin to see things with clarity. The glass isn't meant to be judged; it's meant to be used, appreciated, and understood.

Embracing life "as it is" doesn't mean abandoning hope or caution—it means holding both lightly while standing firmly in truth. This grounded awareness frees us from illusions, allowing us to navigate the ever-changing tides of life with equanimity, presence, and purpose. In this space, we find peace—not by controlling the contents of the glass, but by simply recognizing its existence.

Chapter 19

Excessive Worrying Is an Addiction

A restless mind begins to spin,
Chasing storms that lie within.
What if, what then, what could go wrong?
It sings its anxious, endless song.

We wear it like a heavy coat,
A sinking fear that doesn't float.
Yet most we fear will never be—
Just shadows cast we cannot see.

So, breathe, release, and trust the flow,
Not all is ours to fix or know.
In stillness, peace can reappear—
When love speaks louder than our fear.

Worrying is a deeply ingrained human behavior—an evolutionary response designed to protect us from potential harm. In ancient times, our ancestors relied on this mechanism to anticipate dangers like predators, food shortages, or threats to safety. It was a survival tool, sharpening their senses and responses to secure a better chance at survival.

In our modern world, however, the threats we face are no longer immediate or life-threatening, yet the instinct to worry remains. Today, we worry about finances, relationships, careers, health, and countless unknowns. In many ways, worry offers the illusion of control in the face of uncertainty. It feels like a proactive way to prepare for future challenges. Some even equate worry with responsibility, believing it's a sign of diligence or care. Others subconsciously use worry as a protective mechanism—thinking that by imagining the worst, they might somehow lessen the impact if it happens.

But while occasional worry can help us prepare or problem-solve, excessive worrying tips the balance and becomes maladaptive. It leads to chronic stress, anxiety, emotional fatigue, depression, sleep disturbances, and even physical ailments like a weakened immune system. More dangerously, it can become habitual—an addictive emotional pattern rooted in a false sense of security.

From a spiritual perspective, excessive worry signifies a disconnection from one's higher self or divine source. It reveals a lack of faith in the universe, God, or the natural order of life. When we over-identify with the ego—believing we must control every outcome—we drift further from inner peace and surrender. Many spiritual traditions point to this as a core barrier to growth. In Buddhism, worry is one of the mental hindrances that obstruct clarity and enlightenment. In Christianity, it is often viewed as a sign of distrust in divine providence.

In this light, worry is not just a mental habit—it is a spiritual imbalance. It suggests that we are not aligned with our soul's knowing, that we are operating from fear rather than faith, from control rather than surrender. This misalignment often stems from emotional attachments, unmet expectations, and unhealed traumas that keep the mind restless and afraid.

Moreover, excessive worry can resemble a form of addiction—a "stress addiction." Just like with any other addiction, the brain begins to crave the emotional surge that comes with worry. The body becomes hooked on the adrenaline from the fight-or-flight response. Even when the external situation doesn't call for alarm, the internal chemistry seeks out something to worry about. People may unconsciously create or exaggerate problems simply to feel that familiar rush of alertness. Over time, this cycle becomes deeply ingrained, making it difficult to break free.

Signs that worry may have become a form of addiction include:

- Persistent, daily anxiety over multiple aspects of life
- Inability to disconnect from news or stress-inducing content
- Feeling restless or anxious without access to communication tools or updates
- A tendency to magnify small issues into major concerns
- Immediately replacing a resolved worry with a new one.

To begin releasing this addiction to worry, we can turn to holistic and practical methods that retrain the mind and soothe the nervous system:

- **Cognitive Behavioral Techniques:** Strategies like "worry journaling," setting designated "worry time," or using tools like the "worry tree" help reframe and challenge anxious thoughts.

- **Mindfulness and Presence:** Grounding practices like meditation, conscious breathing, and body awareness can help anchor us in the present moment, reducing the mind's urge to catastrophize.
- **Emotional Support:** Speaking with trusted friends, spiritual mentors, or mental health professionals can provide needed perspective and emotional relief.
- **Spiritual Alignment:** Reconnecting with one's inner self, higher power, or divine purpose through prayer, contemplation, or energy healing can help restore trust in the flow of life.
- **Lifestyle Changes:** Reducing overstimulation, limiting media consumption, spending time in nature, and practicing gratitude can calm the nervous system and reinforce a sense of safety.

Reflective Conclusion

Excessive worrying is more than just a habit—it can become an addiction rooted in fear, ego, and disconnection from the present moment. While it may arise from a desire to protect ourselves or feel prepared, chronic worry ultimately robs us of peace, vitality, and spiritual alignment. Recognizing worry as a form of addiction invites us to approach it with compassion, curiosity, and conscious effort. Through mindfulness, inner healing, and trust in a higher intelligence, we can begin to release our dependence on worry and return to the natural state of calm awareness. In doing so, we reclaim our power—not by controlling life, but by flowing with it.

Chapter 20

The Ego: Servant, Not Master

The ego speaks in voice so loud,
It seeks applause, it seeks the crowd.
But truth is found in softer tone,
The higher self that stands alone.

It plays its part, both sharp and wise,
Yet dims the light behind disguise.
When ruled by fear, it takes control—
But never fills the aching soul.

So let it serve, not lead the way,
A humble guide, not one to sway.
For when the soul begins to sing,
The ego bows—and crowns the King.

In psychology, the ego plays a central role in shaping the human experience. It is often defined as the part of the psyche that mediates between the unconscious drives of the id, the moral constraints of the superego, and the demands of the external world. According to Freud's structural model of the mind, the ego functions on the reality principle—it seeks to satisfy the id's desires in realistic and socially acceptable ways while maintaining a coherent sense of identity. It is the decision-maker, the regulator, and the gatekeeper of conscious experience.

In this technical framework, the ego is vital for psychological balance. It helps us navigate complex social environments, assert our boundaries, develop a personal identity, and function effectively in daily life. Defense mechanisms like denial, repression, or projection are tools it uses to shield the psyche from internal conflict and anxiety. In this sense, the ego is not inherently "bad"—it is a necessary construct for survival and social engagement.

However, in everyday usage and in many spiritual traditions, the term "ego" often carries a more negative connotation. It is associated with self-importance, arrogance, and attachment to form—traits that can distort perception and block spiritual growth. When people speak of someone having a "big ego," they are usually referring to an inflated sense of self, often driven by insecurity, fear, or a desire for validation. In this state, the ego becomes over-identified with roles, titles, accomplishments, or material possessions, clinging to the illusion of separation and superiority.

This over-identification marks a divergence between the healthy function of the ego and its dysfunctional dominance. In spiritual and metaphysical teachings, the ego is not the enemy, but it is not the master either. It is a servant—a tool meant to serve the Higher Mind or Higher Self, which represents the deeper, eternal essence of who we are. The Higher Mind is connected to divine wisdom, intuition, love, and unity consciousness. It transcends the boundaries of time, space, and identity, and acts as the soul's compass toward purpose and authenticity.

When the ego becomes the master, the results are predictable: fear, resistance, conflict, attachment, and a sense of lack. It constructs a reality based on comparison, judgment, and scarcity, blinding us to our true nature. In contrast, when the Higher Mind leads and the ego assumes its rightful role as the servant, life becomes an expression of inner alignment. The ego is no longer driven by the need for control or approval, but by the desire to serve something greater than itself.

The path toward this alignment is not one of ego eradication, but of ego integration. The ego must be educated, not annihilated. It must learn to surrender to the intelligence of the soul. Practices like meditation, mindfulness, conscious breathwork, inner reflection, and shadow work are essential tools in this process. They cultivate self-awareness, allowing us to recognize when the ego is acting from fear and invite us to realign with love, presence, and trust.

Living from the Higher Mind means navigating life with clarity, grace, and a deep sense of purpose. It means making decisions not from reaction, but from response, not from fear, but from wisdom. It is a life where power is internal rather than imposed, where peace is rooted in being rather than having, and where identity is expanded beyond the confines of form.

Reflective Conclusion

The ego, while often misunderstood, is not a flaw in our design—it is a feature. But it is a feature meant to serve, not rule. When it becomes the master, it creates illusions of separation, fear, and limitation. But when guided by the

Higher Self, the ego becomes a powerful ally—a loyal steward of the soul's purpose in this realm.

True freedom arises when we stop identifying with the ego's fleeting sense of self and instead anchor into the enduring truth of our being. We are not merely personalities with roles to play; we are souls on a journey of remembering. In that remembrance, the ego finds peace in its place—not as the center of existence, but as a servant of something far more luminous.

In mastering the ego by allowing it to serve, we step into the wholeness of who we truly are conscious creators, divine beings, and radiant expressions of the infinite.

Chapter 21

Act with Purpose, Not in Desperation

Not from fear, but from the flame,
Let your steps be more than name.
In stillness find your truest guide—
Not chasing lack, but truth inside.
Walk with grace, not haste or race,
For purpose blooms in patient space.

There are moments in life when, caught in the chaos of circumstance or the weight of unmet desires, we find ourselves acting impulsively—without clarity or reflection. These reactions are often rooted in the primal fight-or-flight response, triggered by fear, uncertainty, or the belief that we must urgently attain a particular goal or object to feel whole. In this reactive state, desperation takes the wheel. We cling to the idea that unless we obtain what we desire, we are incomplete. And when the surrounding conditions do not align with our expectations, panic sets in, and we make decisions that may not only derail our progress but compromise our integrity and peace of mind.

Desperation is not born from a place of strength—it stems from fear. It is the fear of separation, the illusion of lack, and the scarcity mindset that convinces us that there is not enough love, success, time, or opportunity. This fear narrows our vision and keeps us tethered to the illusion that external forces dictate our lives, stripping us of agency. We become victims of our own narratives, reacting to life rather than co-creating it.

But we were not made for such limitation. As expressions of the Divine, we carry within us the spark of creative potential—the ability to shape reality with intention, clarity, and love. Our lives are meant to be lived with purpose, guided by an inner compass rooted in our values and soul's wisdom. When we act with purpose, our energy is directed and coherent. We become aligned with the greater rhythm of life, and our actions flow from a place of centeredness and inner knowing.

Purposeful living requires presence. It asks us to slow down, discern what truly matters, and make choices that honor our highest selves. It recognizes that the journey is as important as the destination, and that every step, when taken with awareness, builds a life of meaning, not just achievement. Acting with purpose means embracing the truth that we are not here to survive—desperately grasping for what we think we lack—but to thrive as conscious creators, empowered by the infinite potential within us.

Desperation, on the other hand, contracts our energy. It disconnects us from the flow and rhythm of life, making us reactive rather than responsive. In this state, we are more likely to compromise our values, overlook important details, and make decisions that lead to further confusion or suffering.

To *act with purpose, not in desperation* is to choose creation over reaction, clarity over confusion, faith over fear. It is to align with your soul's calling, even when the path is unclear, because you trust in the divine unfolding of your life. It is recognizing that even in the face of challenge or delay, there is wisdom in the waiting and growth in the journey.

Reflective Conclusion

The Power of Intentional Living

The quality of our life is not determined by how quickly we obtain what we want, but by the integrity and clarity with which we move toward it. Desperation may promise quick relief but often leads to long-term regret. Purpose, on the other hand, offers lasting fulfillment—it is the compass that guides us through uncertainty with trust, patience, and grace.

In every moment, we are offered a choice: to act from fear or to act from love. When we choose purpose, we choose to step into our true power—not as desperate seekers grasping at life, but as aware beings who shape it.

So, breathe, pause, and ask yourself not just *what* you are doing, but *why*. Let your actions be an offering of your highest self—not a reaction to your lowest fear.

Chapter 22

Detachment: Freedom from the Illusion of Control

Let go, and breathe—
the river flows without your will.
No need to chase, no need to grasp,
the world turns soft and still.

We cling to names, to dreams, to roles,
believing we must steer the tide.
But freedom lives in quiet hands,
in stepping back with trust inside.

You are the space behind the thought,
the light that flickers deep within.
Detach, and find the truth you seek—
control was never yours to win.

In this world we live in, we often surround ourselves with people, emotions, relationships, places, and possessions that we believe give meaning to our existence. These attachments, whether tangible or intangible, become extensions of our identity—tools through which we define our purpose and establish significance within the framework of this reality. While attachments can bring comfort and familiarity, they also tether us to a construct that thrives on illusion and impermanence. Whether the attachment appears positive or negative, it creates a form of resistance that impedes our natural state of flow—the unburdened, radiant state of being that reflects our true essence as light energy in its purest form.

Yet resistance itself is not inherently detrimental. Paradoxically, it can serve as a roadmap, guiding us through the terrain of self-discovery. Through resistance, we encounter contrast. Through contrast, we gain clarity. Along the path, we meet fellow travelers—souls who are navigating their own unique journeys. These interactions, intentional or serendipitous, become co-creative endeavors that contribute to our collective expansion of consciousness.

Still, no matter how meaningful or profound an experience may be, its true power lies in allowing it to unfold in divine timing. Like the caterpillar in its cocoon, the transformation into a butterfly cannot be rushed without consequence. Our impatience, often disguised as control, can interfere with sacred processes and hinder rather than hasten growth.

Control, in its most basic sense, refers to the ability to manage or influence outcomes. Biologically, the human nervous system demonstrates how complex and necessary internal control can be: regulating emotions, maintaining homeostasis, coordinating movement, and processing decisions. This internal architecture allows us to navigate the world with both instinct and intention. However, external control—our perceived ability to shape and manage people, events, and circumstances—reveals the illusion at the heart of attachment.

When we feel in control, life seems predictable and manageable. We feel empowered, safe from the chaos of uncertainty. But this sense of control is often rooted in illusion. The more we attempt to grasp at external forces, the more we lose touch with our inner sovereignty. The deeper question arises: *Is control a genuine force, or merely another construct of the mind's desire for certainty and dominance?*

True control exists only within the self. Everything outside of us is influenced by countless variables beyond our command. When we become attached to external outcomes, we unknowingly surrender our inner power. In extreme cases, this attachment can lead to obsession—a state where the object of our attention holds dominion over us. What we believe we control, in truth, begins to control us.

Take, for instance, our relationship with thought. We often believe that by thinking, analyzing, and strategizing, we maintain control. But thought itself can become addictive. The constant stream of mental chatter gives rise to emotions, which in turn shape our perception and manifest our lived reality. In this cycle, we become entangled in the illusion of control.

Mindfulness offers the key to liberation. When we recognize that we are not our thoughts, but rather the awareness observing them, we return to our true center. In this state of presence, we reclaim authentic power—the only control that is ever real. No longer bound by the past or anxious about the future, we act from a place of aligned intention rather than reactive compulsion.

Reflective Conclusion

Detachment is not about disengaging from life but about engaging with it from a place of freedom and clarity. It is the art of loving without clinging, acting without controlling, and being without becoming lost in identity. When we detach, we do not reject the world—we simply refuse to let it define or dominate us. We move with the rhythm of life rather than resisting it. We accept what is, let go of what isn't, and trust in the unfolding of what will be.

In this space of surrendered awareness, we discover that the illusion of control dissolves, and in its place, a deeper truth emerges: We are not here to control life—we are here to *co-create* with it. Detachment is the doorway through which this sacred dance begins.

Chapter 23

Love Without Attachment, Serve Without Expectation

Love that clings is not love true,
It binds the heart in shades of blue.
But love that frees, without demand,
Is light that flows from open hand.

To serve with joy, expect no prize,
Just watch the peace that will arise.
A silent gift, a soul set wide,
With nothing lost, and truth as guide.

No chains, no score, no grand display,
Just love that gives itself away.

True love is unconditional. It flows freely, without demands or dependencies, and rarely does it anchor itself to the object of affection in a possessive way. Attachment, on the other hand, is rooted in fear—fear of loss, fear of inadequacy, fear of not being able to express or receive love fully. But fear is the opposite of love. When fear becomes the governing force behind our emotions, love transforms into something transactional, something objectified. The beloved becomes a possession, an extension of the self, and no longer an autonomous being. In such a dynamic, love begins to serve the ego instead of the ego being in service to love.

All authentic forms of love originate from divine love—pure, expansive, and formless. This divine essence is the source from which all expressions of love emerge. However, when filtered through egoic distortions, this love becomes fragmented reduced to conditional attachments and expectations. Love, in its highest form, is kind, generous, and liberating. It does not seek to own, control, or confine. When love is tainted by the desire to possess or manipulate, it no longer reflects its true nature. It becomes a shadow of itself, entangled in illusion.

Divine love transcends time, form, and space. It is the sacred union between the Divine Masculine and the Divine Feminine within us—the sacred marriage of soul and Source. Love born from this union is creative, harmonious, and life-giving. It births universes and realities anchored in balance. Anything less is an illusion—a product of misinterpreted truths and a distortion of divine energy. This false matrix veils the inner light within each of us and sustains a paradigm of separation and fear.

The highest expression of divine love is **service**—not service to egoic ambition or social validation, but service to truth, unity, and the well-being of all. Serving without expectation mirrors the essence of pure love. It arises from a state of wholeness, not from a desire to gain or to be seen. When we serve with expectations, the ego subtly takes control, glorifying itself in the act of giving and diminishing the purity of the service. Such giving becomes transactional and hollow, eventually leading to frustration and resentment.

To love without attachment is to hold space for another without the need to own, change, or keep them. It means appreciating a person for who they are and honoring their journey, even if it diverges from our own. This love does not seek to mold someone into an ideal nor derive its worth from reciprocation. It allows the other to be free, to change, to come and go. It is rooted in presence, acceptance, and compassion—not in permanence.

To cultivate this kind of love, we must first anchor it within ourselves. We begin by observing our emotions without judgment, becoming aware of where our desire to control or attach arises. We question our impulses and shift our focus from what we can receive to what we can give. We acknowledge that all things, including relationships, are impermanent. And in accepting this, we free ourselves and others to exist in their authentic state.

In parallel, **serving without expectation**—true altruism—is a profound practice of the soul. It means offering our time, talents, and presence with no anticipation of reward or recognition. This kind of service honors the divine spark in others and allows us to align with the higher frequencies of love and compassion. Whether we're volunteering, supporting a friend, or simply doing our daily work, we can perform every act with integrity and wholeheartedness, regardless of who is watching or what we may gain.

This selfless service nourishes both the giver and the receiver. It expands our capacity for love and deepens our connection to the greater whole. When we find fulfillment in the act of giving itself, we begin to mirror the unconditional nature of divine love.

Throughout history, great spiritual teachers have exemplified this path. Figures like Jesus embodied the essence of loving without attachment and serving without expectation. His life was a testament to the power of selfless love and unwavering service—acts not born of need, but of purpose and divine alignment.

Reflective Conclusion

In a world that often equates love with possession and service with validation, choosing to love without attachment and to serve without expectation is a radical act of spiritual maturity. It is a return to the essence of who we are—divine beings capable of expressing pure, limitless love. This path requires awareness, courage, and humility, but it leads to liberation—for ourselves and for others.

When we detach love from fear and expectation, it becomes a sacred offering, a mirror of the divine within. When we serve from a place of wholeness rather than lack, our service becomes a living prayer—one that uplifts the soul and echoes across time and space. In choosing this path, we align with the highest truth: that love, in its purest form, does not seek to possess—it seeks only to bless. And service, in its most divine expression, is the purest form of love in motion.

Chapter 24

Intuition: The Whisper of the Divine Within

A whisper stirs, so soft, so clear,
Not from the mind, but from the sphere
Where soul and silence gently meet—
A truth that reason can't defeat.

No proof it shows, no path it draws,
Just quiet nudges without pause.
Yet when we trust its wordless tone,
We find a wisdom all our own.

Each one of us, to some degree, is gifted with the remarkable ability to understand something immediately, without the need for conscious reasoning—we call this *intuition*. Often described as a gut feeling, a subtle nudge, or an unshakable inner knowing, intuition transcends logic and speaks directly to our deeper awareness. It is that quiet, yet compelling voice within that seems to know the truth before our mind has a chance to analyze or understand.

Intuition manifests in many forms. Spiritual traditions commonly recognize the "Clairs" as expressions of intuitive gifts:

- **Clairvoyance:** Intuitive seeing—receiving visual impressions beyond ordinary perception.
- **Clairaudience:** Intuitive hearing—perceiving sounds or messages internally.
- **Clairsentience:** Intuitive feeling—sensing energy, emotions, or subtle vibrations.
- **Claircognizance:** Intuitive knowing—sudden realizations without logical deduction.
- **Clairalience and Clairgustance:** Less common, involving intuitive smell and taste.

From a psychological perspective, intuition has been categorized into forms such as:

- **Expert Intuition:** Based on deeply internalized experience.
- **Creative Intuition:** Spontaneous and innovative problem-solving.
- **Social Intuition:** Insight into people and relationships.
- **Temporal Intuition:** Timing-related decision-making and foresight.

Philosophers distinguish between **pure intuition**—the innate perception of space and time as universal concepts—and **empirical intuition**, which involves sensory impressions shaped by lived experience.

On a more familiar level, intuition expresses itself as:

- **Gut Feelings:** Instinctive reactions rooted in unconscious pattern recognition.
- **Pattern Recognition:** The rapid identification of familiar dynamics in situations.
- **Inner Insight:** Sudden, wordless clarity or certainty that bypasses logic.

Though subtle, intuition is incredibly powerful. It integrates vast amounts of sensory input, emotional data, and past experiences below the threshold of conscious awareness. What emerges is often a sudden, coherent sense of direction or understanding that may feel more like revelation than reasoning. While some view this process as holistic integration, others interpret it as an unconscious inference that mimics the results of deliberate thought but arrives with astonishing speed.

Unlike rational analysis, intuition does not rely on sequential steps or external proof. It presents itself as an inner certainty—a felt truth. It may arise spontaneously, offering immediate clarity about people, situations, or decisions. At its most profound, it feels like a resonance with something greater than us, as if tapping into a deeper current of wisdom or a universal intelligence.

For those on a spiritual path, intuition is often seen as the voice of the **higher self**, the **soul**, or even the **Divine**. It is not just an internal mechanism of cognition, but a sacred channel of communication between our human experience and our spiritual essence. This is why it is sometimes described as "the whisper of the Divine within." It guides us toward authenticity, truth, and alignment with our soul's purpose—even if the logic behind it is unclear in the moment.

However, it's important to recognize that intuition can be clouded by personal biases, unprocessed trauma, emotional attachments, or fears. These distortions can masquerade as intuitive insight, making discernment essential. Developing a strong, clear connection to intuition requires cultivating presence, self-awareness, and inner stillness. Like a muscle, intuition becomes sharper and more reliable with conscious practice.

One of the most effective ways to strengthen intuition is by learning to trust it. This means honoring those subtle nudges, listening to your body's wisdom, observing recurring dreams or symbols, and giving value to persistent inner messages. The more we validate these inner signals through aligned action, the more confidently intuition speaks.

Reflective Conclusion

Intuition is not merely a mental faculty; it is the sacred language of the soul. In a world often dominated by noise, logic, and distraction, intuition invites us to turn inward, to trust the stillness, and to follow the silent whisper that speaks from the heart of our being. It is both compass and guide, helping us navigate the unseen dimensions of our lives with grace and clarity.

To walk with intuition is to walk in harmony with the Divine within. It is to live with deeper presence, clearer purpose, and an abiding trust in the wisdom that moves through us. When we choose to listen—truly listen—to that inner voice, we begin to align our lives not just with what is reasonable, but with what is *right* for the soul. In honoring intuition, we honor the truth of who we are.

Chapter 25

Impatience: The Urge to Rush Tomorrow

The seed does not demand the bloom,
It rests in silence, space, and room.
The river flows, it does not race,
It trusts the pull of time and grace.

We long to leap, to chase, to know,
But wisdom waits and moves with flow.
What's meant to be will find its way—
Not rushed, not forced, just born one day.

So, breathe, be still, release the climb,
There's sacred power in perfect time.

Impatience is the inner turbulence that arises when life doesn't move at the pace we expect. It manifests as restlessness, irritability, or frustration when faced with delays, obstacles, or unmet desires. At its core, impatience is a visceral discomfort with the present moment—an ache to leap ahead into the future.

The Anatomy of Impatience

Impatience is the absence of patience—an unwillingness to sit with uncertainty or wait with grace. It often shows up as:

- **Restlessness and Irritability:** A racing mind, fidgeting body, or agitation in moments of stillness.
- **Desire for Immediate Gratification:** An internal demand for quick fixes and instant results.
- **Impulsive Behaviors:** Hasty decisions driven by the discomfort of delay.
- **Control and Expectation:** An urgent need to shape outcomes and direct the flow of events.

Though impatience is often perceived negatively, it can also serve as a double-edged sword. In its more constructive form, it can catalyze action, fuel ambition, and spark creative urgency. However, without balance and self-awareness, it easily morphs into anxiety, frustration, or spiritual misalignment.

Root Causes of Impatience

Impatience rarely arises in isolation—it is often the symptom of deeper psychological and spiritual tensions:

- **Fear of Loss or Delay:** A sense of urgency may stem from fear of missing out, not achieving goals, or losing opportunities.
- **Lack of Trust:** When we doubt the natural unfolding of life, we rush, push, and force outcomes.

- **Anxiety Over Control:** Impatience reflects a desire to control that which is uncontrollable—time, people, or divine timing.
- **Cultural Conditioning:** In a world of instant gratification, where responses are measured in seconds and deliveries in hours, slowness feels intolerable.
- **Unrealistic Expectations:** When reality fails to meet our mental timeline, impatience fills the gap with resistance and resentment.

Impatience is not merely a temperament issue; it is often a signal that we are misaligned with the deeper rhythms of life.

Spiritual Implications of Impatience

From a spiritual lens, impatience reveals more than personality—it points to our relationship with time, surrender, and the divine.

1. **Lack of Trust in Divine Timing**

   Impatience subtly implies distrust in God's wisdom and sovereignty. It reflects the belief that unless we interfere or rush the process, things won't work out. This desire to "make things happen" can lead us away from sacred timing and into forced outcomes.

2. **Disruption of Inner Peace and Relationships**

   Hasty actions can cause spiritual setbacks, strained relationships, and inner turmoil. When we act prematurely, we often bypass lessons, opportunities, or blessings that would have unfolded had we waited.

3. **Missed Spiritual Growth**

   Impatience short-circuits transformation. Many of life's most profound awakenings require time—seasons of waiting, enduring, and refining. Impatience tries to bypass this soul-deep alchemy.

4. **Opening to Undesirable Behaviors**

   Complaining, blaming, and acting outside divine will often follow impatience. We murmur when things don't go our way, forgetting that life unfolds with purpose beyond our limited understanding.

The Path to Cultivating Patience

To grow beyond impatience, we must cultivate practices rooted in faith, surrender, and trust:

- **Trust in Divine Timing**: Recognize that delays are not denials. Divine timing is not about convenience but alignment.

- **Seek Inner Stillness**: In moments of waiting, turn inward. Silence, breath, and prayer can transform agitation into peace.

- **Develop Humility:** Accepting that we are not the orchestrators of everything allows us to embrace life as it comes.
- **Practice Perseverance:** Stay the course even when answers or results aren't immediate. Patience is not passive—it is enduring trust in motion.

Reflective Conclusion

Impatience is not merely about waiting—it is about how we wait. Do we wait with clenched fists and anxious hearts, or with open hands and surrendered souls? Every delay is an invitation—to trust more deeply, to love more fully, and to live more presently, to truly enjoy the gifts of the moment which we constantly miss out on.

The future is not a prize to be rushed toward, but a sacred unfolding we are invited to meet with reverence. When we learn to honor the pace of life, we begin to see that each moment holds its own perfection—even the slow ones, even the quiet ones, even the ones that seem like nothing is happening at all.

In truth, the soul does not operate on a clock. It moves in seasons, in tides, in divine rhythms. And the more we attune ourselves to that sacred tempo, the more peace we discover—not just in what's to come, but in what already is.

Let patience not be the absence of desire, but the presence of trust. Let waiting be not a punishment, but a prayer. For in the stillness of waiting, something holy is always being born.

Chapter 26

Divine Timing: The Universe Moves When You're Ready

When all feels slow and dreams delay,
And hope seems just a breath away,
Know life unfolds in perfect grace—
Not lost, not late, just in its place.

The seed must sleep before it grows,
The river waits before it flows.
So, trust the pause, embrace the climb,
For all things bloom in sacred time.

No need to rush, no need to fear,
What's meant for you will soon be near.
The universe moves, calm and wise—
With patient hands and endless skies.

In today's rapidly evolving world, it feels as though time is accelerating. With innovations like high-speed internet, 5G connectivity, and the growing capabilities of artificial intelligence, life seems to unfold at lightning speed right before our eyes. This surge of technological advancement, while beneficial in terms of productivity and efficiency, also fosters an insatiable desire for instant gratification. In the realm of machines, speed is a virtue—but when applied indiscriminately to human life, it can create an unnatural rhythm that undermines the organic unfolding of our personal journeys.

The pressure to keep pace with this "fast-phase" reality often results in feelings of inadequacy, anxiety, or perceived failure if milestones aren't achieved within a predefined timeline. In our rush to accomplish more, we may compromise quality, overlook important details, or disconnect from the relational and emotional aspects that give depth and meaning to our experiences. What was once a journey of presence and purpose becomes a race against time—a race that no one truly wins.

From a human perspective, this constant acceleration can rob us of the richness of the present moment. We are frequently preoccupied with futures that haven't yet arrived or haunted by past mistakes made in haste. We lose the sacredness of *now*, distracted by what *should have been* or *what's next*. Yet, as divine beings experiencing life through human form, our purpose is not to outrun time, but to fully *inhabit* it—to savor, learn, evolve, and align with the deeper currents of our soul's journey.

This brings us to the wisdom of **Divine Timing**—the understanding that everything unfolds at the precise moment it is meant to, not according to our ego's urgency, but in accordance with a greater cosmic plan. Divine timing teaches that life is not random. Events, opportunities, delays, and even detours are woven into the soul's journey with intentionality. What may seem like stagnation, failure, or misfortune from a limited view often carries deeper meaning when seen through the lens of divine orchestration.

Key Aspects of Divine Timing

- **A Higher Plan:**

  Divine timing implies trust in a universal intelligence—God, Source, the Universe—that holds a larger blueprint for our lives. What unfolds is not by accident, but by sacred design.

- **Perfect Timing, Not Immediate Timing:**

  The right thing at the wrong time is still the wrong thing. Divine timing is not about speed, but *ripeness*—like fruit picked in season, it ensures that what arrives is ready, whole, and aligned.

- **Trust and Surrender:**

  Embracing divine timing requires surrendering the illusion of control and trusting that life is unfolding *for* you, even when outcomes appear delayed or uncertain.

- **Catalyst for Spiritual Growth:**

  Every waiting season, delay, or redirection often holds within it a hidden lesson. These moments build character, refine desires, and prepare the soul for what lies ahead.

- **Alignment and Co-Creation:**

  Divine timing does not mean passive waiting. It calls us to align with our truth, take inspired action, and move when intuition nudges, knowing that right effort is guided by right timing.

How to Embrace Divine Timing

- **Be Patient:**

  Understand that the process of becoming and creating is sacred and takes time. Rushing undermines the richness of what is being cultivated.

- **Trust the Process:**

  Even when the path feels uncertain, trust that unseen forces are working on your behalf. Life may be rearranging people, places, or circumstances to make room for your next breakthrough.

- **Take Inspired Action:**

  Don't confuse surrender with inaction. Listen for the inner promptings and take steps with intention and faith, rather than fear or force.

- **Release the Need for Control:**

  The universe operates on laws greater than our schedules. Let go of micromanaging the outcomes and allow grace to move in unexpected ways.

- **Tune Into Your Intuition:**

  Your inner guidance is the compass that keeps you aligned with divine flow. Listen, feel, and honor it.

- **Live in Alignment:**

  When your values, intentions, and actions are in harmony, you become more attuned to divine timing. You recognize synchronicities not as coincidence, but as confirmation.

Reflective Conclusion

Trust the Rhythm of the Soul

Divine timing reminds us that life is not a checklist to be hurried through but a sacred unfolding that requires presence, trust, and soul alignment. When we let go of the artificial deadlines imposed by societal norms or internal fears, we begin to see that nothing is ever late or lost—it is simply becoming, in perfect rhythm with who we are destined to be.

The universe does not respond to desperation; it responds to readiness. When you are aligned in mind, body, and spirit, the doors meant for you will open effortlessly. You will not have to chase what is divinely yours. It will arrive—not early, not late—but precisely when your soul is ready to receive.

So, breathe. Rest. Walk in faith. The timing is divine, and so are you.

Chapter 27

Vibrational Resonance: Secret to Harmony and Balance

Vibrations unseen, yet deeply known,
In every thought, a seed is sown.
The heart, a tuning fork of light,
Resonates with love or fear's bite.

What we emit, we soon attract,
The outer world just echoes back.
A song of peace, a pulse of grace,
Can shift the tone of time and space.

So, tune your soul to higher sound,
Where harmony and truth are found.
In stillness, let your spirit rise,
Aligned with stars, and open skies.

Vibrational resonance occurs when a system is exposed to an external frequency that matches its own natural vibration, resulting in amplified movement. This principle applies not only to mechanical, electrical, or acoustic systems but also to our physical bodies and emotional states. In everyday language, resonance happens when an external vibration matches an object's natural frequency, causing it to vibrate louder. It reflects the core idea that energy, when matched in frequency, amplifies and harmonizes.

At the heart of vibrational resonance lies the **Law of Vibration**, a principle foundational to both science and spirituality. According to this law, everything in the universe is in a state of constant motion. Whether it is physical matter, emotion, or thought, all things are made of energy vibrating at particular frequencies. Even objects that appear solid and motionless are, at the subatomic level, in perpetual vibration.

Thought, as energy, carries its own unique frequency. Just as a radio station emits waves to be received and decoded, our thoughts and emotions transmit vibrational signals into the universe. When we think or feel in higher frequencies—such as love, compassion, gratitude, and peace—we align with the universal flow. In contrast, lower frequencies—like fear, anger, jealousy, and shame—tune us into chaotic, fragmented energies that disconnect us from our true nature. Our task, then, is to become conscious of our inner state and learn to "tune" ourselves to higher vibrational wavelengths.

This is where the **Law of Resonance** comes into play. While the Law of Vibration teaches that everything moves and vibrates, the Law of Resonance tells us that energies of similar frequency are drawn together. Our dominant emotional and mental frequencies act like magnets, drawing experiences, people, and outcomes into our lives that match the vibrational quality of our inner state.

Imagine your mind as a radio tuner. Through deliberate practice—such as meditation, mindfulness, and the use of affirmations—you can adjust the dial of your consciousness to connect with more empowering frequencies. **Meditation** helps quiet the mental noise and makes space for tuning into the higher rhythms of wisdom, clarity, and serenity. **Mindfulness** allows us to become aware of the present moment, gently guiding our thoughts away from fear or judgment and back into alignment with peace. **Affirmations**, when practiced with intention, help retrain the subconscious by embedding high-vibrational beliefs, such as "I am enough" or "I am love."

In therapeutic practices, these ideas are echoed through modalities such as **Vibrational Resonance Therapy (VRT)**. This form of sound healing employs tools like singing bowls, tuning forks, and sound baths to realign the body's natural frequencies. It is believed that specific sound waves can interact with the vibrational frequencies of our cells, promoting healing, emotional release, and balance. The theory is simple: just as dissonance causes tension, harmonious resonance restores order.

Both the Law of Resonance and VRT emphasize the intimate relationship between our inner frequency and our lived reality. Where VRT restores physical and emotional harmony through sound, the Law of Resonance offers a broader energetic perspective: that by aligning our thoughts, emotions, and intentions with higher frequencies, we can transform our personal experience from the inside out.

Reflective Conclusion

In the grand symphony of existence, everything—seen and unseen—is in constant motion, vibrating to its own frequency.

Our lives are not merely shaped by chance, but by the vibrations we emit and resonate with. Whether through conscious thought, emotional attunement, or energetic healing, we are continually creating our reality in resonance with the frequencies we embody.

Understanding vibrational resonance is more than theoretical—it's a call to self-awareness. When we begin to observe the vibrations we carry within, we step into the role of the conscious creator. By tuning into higher frequencies—through love, gratitude, mindfulness, and intentional thought—we not only elevate our personal experience but also contribute to the collective harmony of the world.

Harmony and balance are not destinations we reach but vibrations we choose to sustain. And in every moment, through the choices we make and the energy we carry, we are composing the music of our lives. Let that music be one of healing, alignment, and resonance with the divine rhythm of the universe.

Chapter 28

The Truth Shall Set You Free!

Behind the mask, beneath the veil,
Beyond the stories we regale,
There lies a spark, both fierce and true—
The light of Self that's born in you.

We wore the chains of fear and pride,
Played out the roles where love would hide,
Yet all along, the key was near—
The truth we buried out of fear.

No longer bound by shadowed lie,
We rise as stars in open sky.
For once we see, we cease to flee—
And in that truth...
we're finally free.

The journey of an incarnated soul is, in essence, a return to truth. But this truth is not something newly discovered; rather, it is remembered—recalled from the deep well of inner knowing that has long been buried beneath the rubble of illusion and identity. From the moment of incarnation, the soul begins its experience within a world governed by contrast, duality, and limitation. To navigate this realm, it often adopts a false sense of identity—crafted not from essence but from fear, lack, and separation. This illusion is not accidental; it is a necessary disguise that allows the soul to fully immerse itself in the human condition.

The ego, born of survival instincts and reinforced by societal norms, becomes the face of this false identity. It feeds on scarcity and thrives on the illusion of control. From this reptilian mindset, the soul forgets its boundless nature and gives away its power to external authorities, institutions, and false gods. Life becomes a cautious dance of self-preservation, guided not by inner truth but by outer validation. As a result, we imprison ourselves within invisible walls—constructs of limitation that keep us bound to narratives that no longer serve our evolution.

This self-imposed disempowerment is the great amnesia of the soul.

However, awakening begins when the soul starts to question the validity of these constructs. The stirring of truth is subtle at first—a whisper from within. Through self-inquiry, deep reflection, and healing of karmic wounds—both ancestral and collective—the soul begins to strip away the layers of conditioning that once felt like protection but were, in fact, cages. Every layer shed brings us closer to our essential nature, the divine spark within that has always known its infinite worth.

Paradoxically, this journey to self-realization is not about gaining anything new. Rather, it is the sacred art of letting go—of unlearning, of unbecoming. We begin to reclaim the scattered fragments of our soul that we unknowingly gave away in exchange for acceptance, validation, or love. In doing so, we shift from an outward-driven existence to an inward-directed life. External accolades, attachments, and illusions fall away, and what remains is the unadulterated truth of who we are. And once this truth is known—truly known—there is no going back.

Like light breaking through a dense fog, truth illuminates the darkest corners of our being. It does not just inform; it transforms. The soul becomes radiant, alive, and free. No longer bound by fear or shame, we begin to live with authenticity, guided by inner wisdom and aligned with divine purpose. This truth activates our creative power and reveals our role as co-creators of reality—artists of light shaping form, bringing heaven into the density of earth through the vibration of bliss.

In this liberated state, we do not merely survive—we thrive. Our lives become an expression of divine essence, lived with clarity, intention, and joy. The illusions that once governed us are seen for what they are: lessons, not limitations. The chains fall away, and in their place, wings unfold.

The Biblical Truth and Spiritual Liberation

The phrase *"The truth shall set you free,"* as spoken by Jesus in John 8:32, holds a deep metaphysical and spiritual significance. In its biblical context, the "truth" refers to the knowledge of God's will, the essence of divine nature, and our reconciled relationship with the Divine. It is a call to liberation not merely from external oppression, but from the deeper bondage of sin, ignorance, and spiritual death. It's an invitation to step into the light of divine truth, to be free from illusion, and to live in alignment with divine law.

This liberation is not passive; it is a conscious return to soul awareness. It is the recognition that freedom is not found outside of us, but within—through the realization of our eternal connection to the Divine Source.

Reflective Conclusion

Why Truth Matters

In a world shaped by narratives, illusions, and surface appearances, truth is the rarest and most powerful liberation. It is the compass that guides the soul back to itself. To embrace truth is to dissolve the illusions that once enslaved us. It is to reclaim our divinity, to live as conscious creators rather than unconscious consumers of life.

The relevance of truth today is profound. In a time where information is abundant, but wisdom is scarce, where identity is often shaped by algorithms and projections, the soul longs to remember what is real. And what is real cannot be bought, taught, or imposed—it must be remembered.

Truth does not enslave; it frees. It does not shame; it redeems. It is not rigid dogma; it is living awareness.

To walk in truth is to walk in freedom. And in that freedom, the soul dances—unbound, unafraid, and fully alive.

Chapter 29

Nobody is Your Enemy

No enemy walks beside your way,
Just mirrors dressed in shades of grey.
They poke, they prod, they sometimes sting,
Yet each one comes with truth to bring.

The one who leaves—your strength will show,
The one who mocks—will help you grow.
The one who wounds—invites your grace,
To meet their darkness face to face.

Forgive not just to set them free,
But lift the chains from your own plea.
In every clash, a chance to see,
The soul behind the enmity.

So, bless the ones who test your flame,
They play the part—but not the blame.
In unity, you'll come to see,
There never was an enemy.

Navigating this reality of contrast and duality can be overwhelming, especially for a soul that is still tethered to the limited perception of form. When our awareness is rooted solely in the physical world—governed by survival instincts, rigid beliefs, and the illusion of separateness—life can feel isolating and hostile. From this contracted state of consciousness, the mind operates within a "reptilian" framework: defensive, reactive, and driven by fear. In such a state, it is easy to fall into a victimhood mentality, where the world appears threatening and others seem like enemies out to harm or diminish us.

But this perception is just that—an illusion. It stems not from truth, but from forgetting who and what we truly are.

To the awakened soul—one who recognizes its inherent divinity and connection to all that is—this illusion begins to dissolve. With expanded awareness comes a shift in perspective. From the elevated vantage point of unity consciousness, life is no longer perceived through the lens of fear and separation, but through the lens of oneness and interconnection. The enlightened soul understands that nothing happens *to* us, but rather *for* us. Every challenge, every betrayal, every conflict, and every irritation carry a hidden invitation for inner growth.

In this space of awareness, enemies cease to exist. Instead, we begin to see reflections—mirrors of our own wounds, fears, desires, and lessons. Every interaction, whether pleasant or painful, serves as an opportunity to evolve.

- Those who irritate us are teaching us patience, presence, and emotional regulation.
- Those who abandon us are showing us the strength of self-reliance and the power of standing in our own truth.

- Those who offend us are revealing our capacity for forgiveness and unconditional love.
- That which we fear becomes a teacher of courage and resilience.
- What we cannot control invites us into surrender and trust.
- Rejection teaches us self-worth and independence.
- Problems stimulate innovation and problem-solving skills.
- Criticism sharpens our discernment and calls us to mature responses rather than emotional reactivity.

Life, in its fullness, is a divinely orchestrated classroom—and the people we label as "enemies" are often the greatest catalysts of our awakening. Painful interactions are not indicators of failure, but signs that we are truly participating in life, leaning into growth, and shedding old patterns.

Indeed, if no one ever offends you, disappoints you, or tests you, it could mean you've never taken meaningful risks or lived authentically enough to attract friction. The beauty of this human experience is found in its imperfection. It is in betrayal that we learn trust, in sorrow that we discover depth, and in struggle that we cultivate strength.

Yet, many waste their lives clinging to grudges and feeding resentment—believing that anger punishes the other. But holding onto anger is like drinking poison and expecting someone else to suffer. In truth, the longer we hold onto pain, the longer we delay our own healing and liberation.

Yes, the world is full of difficult people. There will always be those who are rude, careless, or ungrateful. But wisdom lies in how we respond—not in how others behave. Maturity is learning to deal with challenges with grace and detachment. It is realizing that we cannot make everyone like us, think like us, or live like us—and we shouldn't want to. Diversity of thought and behavior is part of the richness of the human tapestry.

Let us learn to forgive—not because others always deserve forgiveness, but because we deserve peace. Let us bury the faults of others and carry forward only what uplifts and refines us. Let us remember that hatred, anger, and intolerance have caused more suffering in this world than any individual ever has. These emotions are thieves that rob us of presence, joy, and purpose.

Reflective Conclusion

In the final analysis, there is no enemy but ignorance—ignorance of who we are, of why we are here, and of the sacredness in others. When we awaken to the truth of our divine essence and the interconnectedness of all life, the concept of "enemy" dissolves into illusion. What remains is compassion—for us and for those still caught in the illusion.

Forgive those who hurt you—not to free them, but to free yourself. Ask for forgiveness where you've caused harm—not out of guilt, but from the wisdom of humility. Life is far too fleeting to waste on vengeance and resentment. At the end of it all, what will matter is not how many battles you fought, but how much peace you brought into the hearts of others.

So, live in such a way that even those who call you an enemy cannot help but respect your light. Transform your wounds into wisdom, your scars into sacred lessons, and your adversaries into unlikely guides. In doing so, you'll realize the profound truth:

Nobody is your enemy—only your teacher.

Chapter 30

Forgiveness: Liberating from Soul Bondage

A burden held, a heavy chain,
A heart once pierced by silent pain.
But in the stillness, soft and deep,
Forgiveness wakes from where we weep.

Not to forget, nor to excuse,
But to reclaim what we might lose—
Our peace, our light, the love we are,
Unbound again like falling star.

So let the wound no longer bind,
Release the past, and free the mind.
For when we choose to set it free,
The first to heal, dear soul, is we.

As spiritual beings incarnated in human form, we experience life through the lens of individuality. This unique sense of self enables us to navigate the physical world, but it also brings us into constant interaction with other souls, each on their own path of growth and awakening. Life, then, is not a solitary journey but a co-creative process—a dynamic exchange of energy between ourselves, others, and the Divine.

In this shared experience, boundaries are tested. As we encounter differences in values, behaviors, and emotional needs, misunderstandings arise. People cross our limits—intentionally or unintentionally—and we may find ourselves feeling disrespected, hurt, or betrayed. These emotional wounds, if left unresolved, fester into bitterness, anger, and resentment. In these moments, the soul becomes entangled in energetic bondage, weighed down by the very pain it longs to escape.

Forgiveness, therefore, becomes not just a moral ideal but a spiritual imperative.

At its core, *forgiveness* is a conscious, intentional act of releasing the grip of resentment or the need for retribution toward someone who has caused harm. It is not about excusing the offense or pretending it never occurred. Rather, forgiveness is about shifting our relationship to the experience—choosing to let go of the emotional poison so we can begin to heal.

Forgiveness is not a passive process. It often requires courage, humility, and the willingness to see beyond the lens of personal hurt. It may involve acknowledging the pain without allowing it to define us and choosing compassion even in the absence of apology or justice. Sometimes, it means surrendering our desire to be understood or validated, recognizing that healing is a gift we give to ourselves, not a reward we offer others.

This sacred process of release unfolds in several dimensions:

- **Letting Go of Retribution:** It's a deliberate choice to no longer wish harm, vengeance, or punishment upon the other person. This is not weakness—it is the strength to break the karmic cycle of "an eye for an eye."

- **Accepting the Past:** Acceptance does not mean agreement or approval. It means no longer fighting what has already occurred, which frees the energy previously trapped in resistance.
- **Seeing the Humanity in the Other:** Even when someone has wronged us, they are still a soul on their journey—perhaps acting from their own wounds, ignorance, or pain. Recognizing their humanity allows for empathy, even if trust is not restored.
- **Choosing Present Peace Over Past Pain:** By not allowing the past to dictate the quality of our present or future, we reclaim our power and inner sovereignty.

Forgiveness extends beyond our relationships with others. **Self-forgiveness** is equally essential. We often carry guilt, shame, and regret for our own actions, choices, or perceived failures. This inner judgment can be just as imprisoning as external blame. True liberation arises when we offer ourselves the same grace we extend to others—acknowledging our imperfections without allowing them to overshadow our divine essence.

From a spiritual perspective, **unforgiveness is a form of soul bondage.** It entangles us in lower vibrational states—anger, resentment, victimhood—that obscure our connection to

Source and distort our perception of self and others. These heavy energies act like chains around the heart, preventing us from fully experiencing love, peace, and wholeness. Forgiveness is the key that unlocks those chains, allowing divine energy to flow freely through our being once again.

Forgiveness restores balance. It doesn't require reconciliation with the person who caused harm, but it *does* require reconciliation with the self. It invites us to remember who we truly are—beings of love, light, and compassion—and to act from that remembrance rather than from the wounds of the ego.

Reflective Conclusion

Forgiveness is not the easy path, but it is the freeing one. When we forgive, we reclaim our spiritual authority, dissolve karmic entanglements, and open our hearts to grace. We no longer allow the pain of the past to define our story. Instead, we transmute that pain into wisdom, compassion, and strength.

To forgive is to say: *"I choose freedom over fear, peace over pain, love over bitterness."*

It is a courageous act of inner alchemy—transforming suffering into liberation.

Let us remember that forgiveness is not a favor we do for others, but a divine offering we give ourselves. It is the soul's declaration that it will no longer be held hostage by hurt, but will rise, unshackled and whole, into the fullness of its light.

In choosing forgiveness, we choose to *be free.*

Chapter 31

Our Choices: Our Prayers

Each step we take, each path we choose,
A silent prayer the soul lets loose.
Not just in words, but in our deeds,
We plant the roots of future seeds.

A whispered thought, a kind embrace,
A moment's pause, a slower pace—
These speak as loud as bowed-down knees,
They echo through eternity's breeze.

So let your choices be sincere,
A prayer in motion, bold and clear.
For Heaven hears not just our pleas,
But how we live our silent creeds.

Prayer is more than a ritual; it is the soul's language—a sacred communication with the Divine. Whether spoken aloud, whispered in silence, or felt through the heart, prayer is a means of expressing gratitude, seeking help, or simply yearning for connection with something greater than ourselves. Across religions and spiritual traditions, prayer takes many forms—from structured liturgy to spontaneous utterances, from collective rituals to quiet, personal reflections. Regardless of its form, prayer is always rooted in intention.

Choices, on the other hand, are the everyday expressions of our will. They represent the intersection of thought, intention, and action. Choices arise in all facets of life—from what we eat, to whom we associate with, to how we respond in moments of challenge. They may seem trivial or monumental, but every choice carries with it a resonance that echoes beyond the moment it is made.

To view **our choices as prayers** is to understand that each decision we make is a declaration of what we value, who we are becoming, and what we align with. Just as a prayer seeks divine guidance, our choices reflect our inner compass—our hopes, fears, desires, and beliefs. In this light, a choice is not just a preference or a response to circumstance, but a sacred act, a manifestation of inner intention projected into the world.

This perspective invites a deeper level of awareness and responsibility. If every choice is a prayer, then every moment is an altar, and every action becomes an offering. This means that what we choose to say, do, believe, or pursue carries spiritual weight. It is not only about what we ask from the Divine, but what we *offer* through our daily decisions.

Whether we consciously realize it or not, we are constantly co-creating our reality through choice. And just as we seek guidance through prayer, our choices, too, become vehicles for aligning with divine will. They serve as active demonstrations of our trust, our values, and our vision of the good. In many spiritual paths, including the Islamic tradition of *istikharah*, this alignment is made explicit choices are not made hastily, but with prayerful reflection, inviting divine clarity into the process.

Reflective Conclusion

To live as though our choices are prayers is to live with intention, reverence, and humility. It is to recognize that each decision, no matter how small, has the potential to shape our path and the world around us. It calls us to pause before we act, to ask not only "What do I want?" but also "What am I truly aligning with?"

When our choices become conscious prayers, life itself becomes a sacred dialogue—one where we do not merely *ask* for blessings but *become* the blessing through the lives we choose to lead.

In this sacred view of decision-making, we are reminded that the Divine listens not only to our words, but to our choices. Let us then choose wisely, for in doing so, we are praying with our lives.

Chapter 32

Karma is Not the Prison—Ignorance Is

Karma weaves a silent thread,
Through every thought and word, we've said.
Not to punish, not to bind,
But to reflect the state of mind.

Yet blind we walk through cause and claim,
Repeating patterns, shifting blame.
Not fate, but fog within our view—
It's ignorance that chains us true.

Awake, and see with clearer eyes,
That every fall can help us rise.
For freedom waits, not far, but near—
In truth remembered, crystal clear.

Karma, a foundational principle in Hinduism and Buddhism, refers to the universal law of cause and effect. It teaches that our actions, thoughts, and intentions inevitably shape our present and future experiences. It's the age-old wisdom captured in the saying, "What goes around, comes around." But karma is far more than cosmic justice or reward and punishment—it is a mirror of consciousness and intention.

At its core, karma emphasizes that every action—whether physical, verbal, or mental—ripples through the fabric of existence, eventually returning to its source. In traditions that embrace reincarnation, karma governs the quality and circumstances of future lives. Good intentions and compassionate actions generate positive karma, while actions rooted in harm or selfishness contribute to future suffering. However, karma is not an external force that punishes or rewards; it is a neutral law of balance that responds to our choices with precision and intelligence.

Importantly, karma works hand in hand with free will. While past actions have laid the foundation for our current experience, we are not bound by them. At any moment, we can choose to act with awareness, integrity, and love—thereby transforming the trajectory of our lives. Karma is not destiny etched in stone; it is the unfolding consequence of choices made and the powerful invitation to choose consciously again and again.

What truly binds us is not karma—it is ignorance.

Ignorance, particularly spiritual ignorance, is the true prison of the soul. It is the absence of understanding about the divine laws that govern life, including karma itself. It is the blindness to our own divine nature, the unconscious adherence to limiting beliefs, and the failure to recognize the sacred interconnectedness of all things.

Spiritual ignorance manifests as a disconnection from truth, an inability to perceive spiritual realities, and resistance to inner growth. It leads to fear-based decisions, confusion between right and wrong, and entrapment in cycles of suffering that could otherwise be transcended. Without awareness, we unknowingly repeat the same mistakes, accumulating consequences not out of malice but out of unconsciousness.

In many traditions, ignorance is considered the root of all suffering. It is not merely a lack of factual knowledge but a profound forgetfulness of who we truly are. When we forget our divine identity and the creative power of our thoughts and intentions, we become slaves to our own illusions. It is ignorance—not karma—that makes us feel powerless, victimized, or lost.

True spiritual liberation begins with awareness. Through study, reflection, prayer, meditation, and direct inner experience, we begin to pierce the veil of ignorance. We come to understand that karma is not punishment but a sacred feedback system guiding us toward alignment with higher truths. It is through this understanding that we reclaim our power as co-creators of our destiny.

To know karma is to awaken responsibility. To transcend ignorance is to step into freedom.

Reflective Conclusion

Karma is not the jailer—it is the teacher. It patiently echoes the choices we make, offering us lessons in growth, compassion, and self-awareness. But without understanding, we misinterpret its messages. We curse our circumstances without recognizing the seeds we ourselves have sown.

It is ignorance—not karma—that shackles us. Ignorance keeps us bound to cycles of pain, illusion, and disempowerment. When we awaken to the truth of who we are—eternal souls capable of wisdom, love, and transformation—we begin to navigate karma with clarity and grace.

The prison walls fall when knowledge dawns. With each conscious choice, we write a new script for our future. We become participants in a divine dance, where karma no longer feels like fate, but like a compass—guiding us back home to our truest self.

In truth, karma does not enslave us. It is ignorance that does. And it is wisdom that sets us free.

Chapter 33

Divine Love: True Measure of Generosity

Love that flows without demand,
Not clenched in grasp, nor tight in hand.
It gives with grace, it shines, it frees—
Like sunlight kissing quiet seas.

No barter made, no score to keep,
It sows in joy; it gives in deep.
The soul that loves with open hand
Reveals the touch of God's own plan.

For love that gives and asks no prize
Reflects the truth beyond the skies:
That in the gift, the giver grows—
And through the heart, Divine Love flows.

What is love?

Love is one of the most profound and multifaceted human experiences. It manifests as deep affection, emotional connection, and an earnest desire for another's well-being. It spans a spectrum of expressions—from passionate attraction to nurturing concern. Yet beyond these personal and emotional dimensions lies **spiritual love:** a transcendent force that connects souls through a shared sense of unity, compassion, and selfless service. This divine expression of love reflects a relationship not only with others but also with the sacred—one that prioritizes giving over receiving, and unity over separation.

However, when love becomes entangled with **attachment**, its essence is often diluted. Attachment is born out of a need for security, reassurance, and belonging. It is deeply shaped by one's early experiences and emotional conditioning. In romantic or personal relationships, attachment can become a lens through which we seek validation, comfort, and identity. It subtly transforms love into a transactional dynamic—one concerned more with what we can receive than what we can give. In its extreme, attachment leads to possessiveness, control, and even greed—turning love inward toward the self, rather than outward in service.

True love, especially divine love, is the antithesis of attachment. Where attachment clings, **divine love liberates**. Where attachment seeks return, **divine love gives freely**. This is the love that is generous at its core—unconditional, expansive, and radiant. It is not bound by expectation or limited to personal gain. Rather, it is an act of **grace**—a reflection of the sacred within us, flowing effortlessly toward others.

In this light, **generosity becomes the natural expression of divine love**. It is not merely the offering of resources, time, or effort. It is the act of giving from the fullness of one's heart, without the anticipation of reward. This spiritual generosity aligns with the principle of *nishkam karma*—selfless action, performed without attachment to outcome. Whether through compassion, forgiveness, presence, or service, divine generosity mirrors the boundless love of God, who gives without measure.

This kind of giving transforms both the giver and the receiver. It is not just an act—it is a sacred transmission. In giving what is most precious, we transcend the ego and draw closer to the divine. As spiritual traditions across the world affirm—from the *Bhagavad Gita* to the Bible—**a cheerful and selfless giver is one who walks with God.** When we extend ourselves in love and generosity, we not only uplift others but align ourselves with the abundant nature of the universe.

Reflective Conclusion

True generosity is not a measure of what we give, but of how we give. It is the love behind the gesture, the intention behind the offering, and the spirit that moves through the act. Divine love, in its purest form, asks for nothing in return. It overflows from a heart that has touched the eternal and seen the sacred in all. In giving selflessly—whether love, time, or kindness—we participate in a divine exchange, one that nourishes both soul and spirit. To love generously is to live abundantly. And in that sacred space of giving, we find ourselves closest to the heart of the Divine.

Chapter 34

Presence: Seat of True Power

In the hush between each breath,
Where past and future lose their depth,
There lies a flame, both still and bright—
The present, wrapped in silent light.

Not in the echoes left behind,
Nor dreams the restless heart may find,
But here and now, the soul draws near—
The voice of truth becomes most clear.

No need to chase, no need to flee,
The moment holds what's meant to be.
For in this pause, both soft and grand,
We touch the pulse of life firsthand.

To be present is to be fully alive. It means to immerse oneself entirely in the here and now, engaging wholly with the current moment rather than lingering in the echoes of the past or projecting into the uncertainties of the future. Presence is not a passive state, but a powerful act of awareness—a conscious decision to meet life as it unfolds, without distraction or resistance.

In its simplest form, presence is mindfulness in action. It involves giving undivided attention to what is directly in front of us—whether that's the taste of a meal, the sound of wind moving through trees, or the subtle rhythm of our own breathing. It invites us to notice not just what we're doing, but *how* we're doing it, moment by moment. This cultivated attentiveness shifts our awareness from habitual autopilot to intentional living.

When we are truly present, the mind becomes clear and anchored. We cease ruminating on the past—what could have been, should have been, or was. We also release the anxious grasping at the future—what might happen or what must be done. Instead, we arrive in the now, where life is actually happening. And in that space, we discover calm, clarity, and inner strength.

This state of presence is not only therapeutic, but transformative. It nurtures emotional intelligence by helping us acknowledge our emotions without being consumed by them. We begin to recognize patterns, self-regulate more effectively, and make choices that are aligned with our values rather than reactive impulses. In presence, stress lessens, focus sharpens, and gratitude deepens.

Moreover, presence strengthens our relationships. In a world saturated with digital noise and perpetual busyness, offering our full attention to another person is a rare and sacred act. Whether it's a loved one, a client, or a stranger, people can feel when we are truly *with* them—not just physically, but mentally and emotionally. This genuine presence fosters trust, deepens intimacy, and nourishes the unspoken threads that bind us together.

Being present is also foundational to personal empowerment. The present moment is the only moment in which we have agency. We cannot alter the past, and we do not control the future. Our only true point of influence is now. Every decision, every transformation, every act of courage or kindness must begin here. As Eleanor Roosevelt aptly said, *"Yesterday is history, tomorrow is a mystery but today is a gift—that's why it's called the present."*

Still, cultivating presence is not always easy. It requires practice, patience, and self-compassion—especially in a culture that glorifies multitasking and productivity. Many of us struggle with feeling insufficiently prepared, especially in roles where we support others. But presence is not about perfection; it is about authenticity. It is the quiet confidence of showing up, just as we are, and offering our full attention with humility and heart.

Reflective Conclusion

Presence is not just a state of mind—it is the very foundation of our power. It is where clarity arises, healing begins, and transformation unfolds. In presence, we reclaim ourselves from the fragmentation of time and distraction, and we return to the sacred fullness of now.

To live present is to live empowered—not by force, but by awareness. In presence, we discover not just peace, but purpose. We meet life not as an observer or a reactor, but as a conscious participant in the unfolding miracle of existence.

The present moment is not merely something to pass through—it is the portal through which all true living begins. And in embracing it, we uncover the timeless truth: that the power we seek has always been right here, within us, now.

Chapter 35

Do Not React, Respond with Awareness

In moments tense, when tempers flare,
Pause and breathe the sacred air.
Let not the storm within decide—
Choose the stillness deep inside.

Reactions rush, like winds that spin,
But wisdom waits and looks within.
With mindful heart and soul intact,
Respond with grace—don't just react.

For power lies in silent space,
Where ego yields to higher grace.
In calm replies, the truth is shown—
Awareness speaks, and peace is grown.

To react means to behave in a particular way in response to a stimulus. In today's world, where we are constantly bombarded by information, emotions, and external pressures, our natural instinct is to react—often impulsively. As sentient beings capable of thought and feeling, we respond to these stimuli based on how they resonate with our understanding or provoke our emotions. Often, these reactions are reflexive, rooted in our survival instincts. They serve to protect us, but they rarely represent our highest self. In such moments, we often fail to pause, reflect, and view the situation from a higher perspective.

From a spiritual standpoint, reacting without awareness can perpetuate cycles of suffering. True spiritual growth invites us to move beyond knee-jerk reactions and instead respond with intention and wisdom. Responding means choosing our behavior based on inner clarity, rather than being swept away by emotional turbulence or external influence. It means aligning our actions with our values, responding to life with compassion, presence, and consciousness.

Responding with awareness is a mindful practice. It calls us to observe our emotional state, recognize the forces that are influencing us, and evaluate the circumstances with both empathy and discernment. Rather than jumping to conclusions or retaliating from a place of pain or ego, we are invited to pause. In this sacred pause, we gather ourselves. We breathe. We consider not only our own emotional responses but also the needs and perspectives of others involved.

This level of awareness can be cultivated through spiritual disciplines such as mindfulness, meditation, prayer, and reflection. These practices anchor us in the present moment, helping us discern the truth beyond emotional chaos. They open space for intuition, inner guidance, and divine wisdom to emerge. In doing so, we become less reactive and more responsive—less controlled by circumstance and more empowered by intention.

Responding with awareness also involves letting go—of expectations, of attachments to outcomes, of the illusion that control equals peace. It calls for radical acceptance of what is, trusting that every situation, however challenging, carries within it a lesson or a blessing. Rather than resisting what unfolds, we surrender with grace and respond with love.

"Respond, don't react" is more than advice—it is a spiritual invitation. It urges us to move from ego to essence, from chaos to clarity, from survival to soulful living. Reacting is instinctual; responding is intentional. Reactions are born of emotion; responses are rooted in awareness.

When we respond with awareness, we cultivate emotional intelligence and inner strength. We communicate more clearly, connect more deeply, and create outcomes that foster healing rather than harm. We transcend momentary impulses and embody presence. In doing so, we honor our highest self and the divine intelligence flowing through all things.

Reflective Conclusion

In the quiet space between stimulus and response lies our greatest power—the power to choose who we become in every moment. Life will continue to challenge us, to trigger us, to provoke reactions. But it is in how we respond that we shape our reality. To respond with awareness is to act from our soul rather than our shadow. It is to become a conscious participant in the unfolding of our lives. It is a sacred practice that, over time, transforms not only our relationships with others but our relationship with ourselves and with the Divine. In this conscious choosing, we discover peace—not as something we find, but as something we become.

Chapter 36

Perfection in Our Imperfection

A crack runs deep across the soul,
Yet still, the heart beats strong and whole.
Not flawless light, but fractured grace—
A sacred fire time can't erase.

We fall, we rise, we mend, we grow,
Through every scar, the truth will show.
For even stars must break the night,
To cast their glow and birth their light.

So let each flaw be not disguise,
But windows where our courage lies.
Divine we are, yet human still—
Perfect in our flawed free will.

At the very core of our being lies an essence that is whole, complete, and perfect—a spark of the Divine that lacks nothing and knows no limitation. This essence is timeless, formless, and eternal. Yet, in our soul's courageous journey through the universe, we made the sacred decision to incarnate into this dense, three-dimensional reality. We willingly entered the realm of contrast and duality, a place where the soul can experience what it cannot in its original perfect form: the taste of limitation, the texture of imperfection, the pressure of polarity, and the depth of emotional experience. This Earthly realm is not a punishment or a fall from grace—it is the ultimate playground for expansion.

Upon arrival in this physical world, we adopt a human form, a vessel that comes with biological needs, mental filters, and emotional programming. We begin to wear masks—false identities shaped by family, culture, religion, and society. We are taught who we should be, how we should act, and what success or value looks like. The brilliance of our Divine essence becomes veiled beneath layers of fear, doubt, shame, and the illusion of separation. And as we buy into this illusion, we begin to experience ourselves not as infinite beings but as fractured, imperfect entities stumbling through life trying to measure up.

This mask of imperfection, however, is not a flaw in the system. It is the very design of the game. The contrast between our divine origin and our earthly experience is not a problem to be fixed—it is a mystery to be lived. In this duality, we encounter not only joy and connection but also heartbreak, failure, and fear. We experience both the heights of ecstasy and the valleys of despair. Each experience, no matter how painful or messy, is a portal to deeper self-awareness and spiritual maturity. This is the sacred paradox of human life: we are perfect beings journeying through the illusion of imperfection for the sake of growth, wisdom, and the expansion of consciousness.

The Gift of Imperfection

To be imperfect is not a sin—it is a sacred opportunity. The saying "Nobody is perfect" is not just a cliché; it is a profound truth wrapped in humility. We are not meant to be flawless, because flawlessness leaves no room for transformation. It is through our perceived flaws that we are invited to evolve, to reflect, to understand, and to awaken. Our mistakes become teachers. Our failures become guideposts. Our wounds become entry points for compassion—both for ourselves and for others.

Too often, we carry our imperfections as burdens, as shameful markers of inadequacy. But what if we switched the narrative? What if we began to see our imperfections not as signs of brokenness but as the very brushstrokes of our unique masterpiece? Rather than resisting or concealing these aspects of ourselves, we can embrace them, learn from them, and allow them to infuse our life with depth, character, and authenticity.

The journey of life is not about arriving at a state of perfection—it is about unfolding, layer by layer, into deeper expressions of our truth. Our imperfections are the very grit that polishes the gem of our soul. They test our courage, stretch our capacity for love, and deepen our empathy for others. Without them, our human experience would be flat, colorless, and devoid of the rich narrative that defines the soul's growth.

Consciousness Through Contrast

One of the most profound reasons we incarnate into this reality is to experience contrast. Contrast is the foundation of awareness. We understand light because we have known darkness. We appreciate peace because we have felt chaos. We cherish joy more deeply after we have tasted sorrow. The full spectrum of human emotions and experiences is what allows consciousness to expand.

In a realm where everything was perfect and complete, there would be nothing to strive for, nothing to create, and nothing to learn. There would be no longing, no aspiration, and no inspiration. Perfection, in that sense, would be a kind of stagnation. It is the illusion of lack that drives desire. It is the sense of separation that drives connection. It is the awareness of imperfection that catalyzes growth. And so, in this divine play, we have agreed to forget our perfection temporarily so that we might remember it in a new way—through experience, through choice, through the beauty of becoming.

The Masterpiece Within the Mess

Human life is messy. It is unpredictable, inconsistent, and often chaotic. We lose our way, we make poor choices, we hurt others, and we hurt ourselves. But embedded within the chaos is a deeper order—one that is orchestrated by the soul for the purpose of awakening.

Think of the greatest works of art, literature, or music. What makes them compelling is not their perfection but their rawness, their emotional depth, and their humanity. In the same way, our lives are not meant to be pristine, flawless performances. They are meant to be works of art—dynamic, textured, layered, and deeply personal.

Our scars tell stories of resilience. Our vulnerabilities allow others to connect with us more authentically. Our willingness to be seen in our imperfection invites others to drop their masks and meet us in the space of realness. In this way, our imperfection becomes the bridge to community, to healing, and to love.

Divine Power in Human Limitations

Despite the limitations of this earthly construct, we carry within us the essence of divine power. We are creators at our core, and even within the narrow confines of human experience, we manifest beauty, innovation, and love. We write poetry, compose symphonies, build civilizations, nurture families, and perform acts of courage and kindness that ripple through the collective.

It is precisely because of our imperfections that we can demonstrate strength, grace, and resilience. When we fall and rise again, when we love despite fear, when we forgive the unforgivable, we activate divine qualities within us. We become living expressions of sacred energy moving through form. We are not limited by our imperfections—we are empowered by them. They give us the raw material from which to craft a life of meaning.

A Call to Self-Acceptance

To see perfection in our imperfection is to recognize the sacredness of where we are right now. It is to stop waging war against ourselves, and to begin the process of reconciliation. This doesn't mean that we stop striving, growing, or healing. It means that we no longer do so from a place of shame or unworthiness, but from a deep reverence for who we are and what we are becoming.

Self-acceptance is a radical act of spiritual defiance in a world that constantly tells us we are not enough. When we accept our imperfections, we reclaim our power. We align with the

Divine design that celebrates uniqueness, honors the process, and trusts the unfolding.

And in doing so, we begin to extend the same compassion and acceptance to others. We stop expecting perfection from our loved ones, our partners, our leaders, or our communities. We recognize that everyone is navigating their own complex journey, filled with lessons and struggles we may never fully understand. Imperfection becomes a shared human bond—one that invites empathy and forgiveness.

A Reflection on the Divine Journey

At the highest level of awareness, perfection is not about flawlessness—it is about harmony. It is about each piece playing its role in the grand symphony of life. Even the dissonant notes, the mistakes, the failures—they all serve a purpose in the orchestration of growth.

To embrace perfection in our imperfection is to trust that nothing is wasted. No experience is meaningless. Every emotion felt, every tear shed, every stumble taken—each one is a brushstroke in the divine artwork of your soul's evolution.

Our return to our Divine self is not a reward for perfection. It is the natural homecoming of a soul that has dared to experience life in its fullest expression. The Divine does not judge your imperfection. It celebrates your courage. It does not measure your worth by your achievements but by your willingness to be present, to love, to learn, and to rise again.

Reflective Conclusion

The Beauty of Becoming

In the end, it is not perfection that makes us divine—it is the journey through imperfection that reveals our divinity. The cracks in our armor allow the light to shine through. The broken pieces of our past become the mosaic of our future. The longing, the loss, the laughter, and the love—all of it is sacred.

We are not here to escape our imperfections but to embrace them as portals of transformation. To understand that this moment—no matter how flawed or painful—is exactly where we are meant to be. It is in this moment that we meet God, not as a distant force, but as the presence within our breath, our tears, and our triumphs.

So let us no longer strive to be perfect in the eyes of the world. Let us instead be perfectly human—raw, real, radiant in our imperfections. Let us live boldly, love deeply, forgive freely, and trust endlessly. For in doing so, we honor the Divine not by being flawless, but by being fully, beautifully, unapologetically ourselves.

Chapter 37

Joy: The Greatest Expression of Divine Alignment

Joy is not a fleeting flame,
Nor bound to fortune, praise, or name.
It rises from the soul's deep well,
Where truth and love in silence dwell.

It dances not on outward gain,
But sings through loss, and shines through pain.
A sacred pulse, a silent guide,
Where Spirit and the self-abide.

When we align with Source above,
Our steps are lit by light and love.
And joy becomes the sacred art—
Of living from a faithful heart.

Joy is often defined as a feeling of great pleasure or happiness, yet it is true essence runs far deeper. Authentic joy is not merely a transient emotion sparked by external events; it is a profound, enduring state of being—a soul-level resonance that emerges from within. It's the unmistakable feeling of being connected, whole, and alive, regardless of circumstances. Joy is not dependent on what happens around us but rather flows from alignment with who we truly are.

Unlike fleeting happiness, which tends to be circumstantial, joy arises from inner peace, gratitude, and a deep-rooted sense of purpose. It is the quiet confidence that comes from knowing and trusting your path, even amid uncertainty or pain. Joy can be found in moments of stillness, in relationships that nourish the soul, in acts of kindness, or in the recognition of beauty and meaning in everyday life.

True joy is not just an emotional experience—it is also a perspective, an orientation toward life that values presence, appreciation, and authenticity. It is cultivated through an intentional attitude of gratitude, mindful awareness, and openness to the present moment. Through joy, we access resilience. We uncover the ability to endure hardship with grace and to find light even in darkness.

In this sense, joy is much more than an emotional uplift—it becomes a spiritual compass. It reveals when we are in alignment with our higher self, our divine source, and our soul's purpose. Spiritual alignment means living in harmony with our core values and divine truth, where our thoughts, emotions, and actions are congruent with our authentic self and with the will of the Divine.

This state of alignment is dynamic, not static. It unfolds as we listen deeply to our inner guidance, pay attention to divine signs, and walk in trust—step by step—with life's unfolding journey. Whether seen as aligning with God, Source, or the rhythm of the universe, the experience is the same: a sense of peace, flow, and clarity.

When we live in this state of divine alignment, joy naturally arises. That joy, in turn, elevates our frequency. Energetically, joy and love vibrate at some of the highest levels, resonating with the frequency of the Divine. When we live joyfully, we open our hearts wide—to receive, to give, and to be transformed. Joy makes us receptive to abundance. It makes us aware of the blessings we might otherwise overlook and transforms ordinary moments into sacred encounters.

Moreover, joy is not solitary—it's contagious. It ripples outward, inspiring others, uplifting environments, and contributing to the healing of the world. A joyful soul becomes a beacon, a transmitter of divine light. In living joyfully, we not only fulfill our own soul's calling—we give permission for others to do the same.

Reflective Conclusion

Joy is the unmistakable signpost of spiritual alignment. It is the Divine whisper saying, *"You are on the right path."* When we follow the trail of joy, we are led closer to our true self and to Source itself. In choosing joy—not just as a fleeting mood but as a way of life—we align with the highest expression of our being. We become vessels of love, magnets for abundance, and instruments of healing in a world that desperately needs light.

Let joy not be the reward of arrival, but the companion of our journey. For in joy, we remember who we are: radiant expressions of the Divine, co-creating a life of purpose, peace, and profound alignment with all that is sacred.

Chapter 38

Magnetism: Preserving Your Energy Field

A field unseen, yet strong and wide,
Protects the soul that dwells inside.
With every thought, with every breath,
We weave our shield, our fate, our depth.

We draw to us what we emit—
The light we shine, the truths we sit.
When hearts are clear and minds aligned,
The world reflects our inner kind.

So, guard your spark, let shadows pass,
Don't wear what's not your soul's own mask.
Through calm and chaos, choose what's true—
Your energy returns to you.

We exist in a universe governed by the fundamental principles of energy and vibration. At our core, we are beings of light—constantly receiving, transmitting, and exchanging energetic frequencies. The nature of our external reality often mirrors our internal state; we attract people, experiences, and circumstances that align with the energy we emit. This unique energetic signature radiates from our personal energy field, reflecting our essence and influencing how we engage with the world.

Our energy field functions like a semi-permeable membrane—meant to protect, filter, and preserve our integrity. When it is strong and intact, it can discern which energies are beneficial and which are harmful. But as we move through life, engaging with various people and environments, entertaining thoughts, and processing emotions, this protective field can become weakened or distorted. The constant bombardment of external energies can leave us feeling scattered, drained, and even burdened by emotions or energies that are not our own.

Such energetic vulnerabilities may lead to confusion, disconnection, and in some cases, dis-ease—manifesting not just physically, but mentally and spiritually. We may unknowingly carry the energetic residue of others, becoming entangled in karmic patterns that do not belong to us. Some individuals, often unaware, act as energy parasites—draining vitality from those around them, simply because they too have failed to safeguard their own fields.

The concept of spiritual magnetism rests on the belief that like attracts like. When our energy field is balanced and positive, we draw in experiences that are harmonious, fulfilling, and aligned with our higher purpose. Conversely, a field clouded by negativity or unresolved emotions can attract chaos, conflict, or stagnation.

To preserve and strengthen our energy field, we must adopt intentional practices that nurture our inner light. Meditation, mindful living, and conscious interactions are foundational. These create the space to ground ourselves, clear mental clutter, and reconnect to our center. Physical health is equally important—proper nutrition, movement, and rest directly influence our energetic stability. Visualization techniques, mantras, chanting, and even biomagnetic therapy can further enhance energetic awareness and protection.

Equally vital is the setting of clear energetic boundaries. This includes learning when to say no, distancing ourselves from toxic influences, and being vigilant of emotional entanglements that drain us. Cultivating a resilient sense of self and projecting energy consciously with awareness and intention enables us to stand in our power, rather than be swayed by external currents.

Reflective Conclusion

Preserving your energy field is not merely a spiritual practice—it is an act of self-respect and conscious living. When we honor our energetic boundaries and strengthen our inner magnetism, we become radiant forces of light, capable of transforming not only our own lives but also the collective field around us. In a world of unseen influences, cultivating a clear, grounded, and vibrant energy field is one of the most empowering gifts we can offer ourselves. It is through this magnetism that we not only protect our essence, but also attract the people, experiences, and opportunities that truly resonate with our soul's journey.

Chapter 39

What the Mind Suppresses, the Body Expresses

Unspoken thoughts, emotions deep,
Don't disappear—they only sleep.
They stir beneath the flesh and bone,
In aching limbs, their truth is shown.

A silent grief, a stifled cry,
Becomes the pain we can't deny.
The body speaks in whispered strain,
What the mind has numbed with hidden pain.

But healing comes when we give voice,
To feel, to face, to make a choice—
To listen close to what it says,
And free the wounds of yesterdays.

So let the heart and body share,
The truths too long we didn't dare.
For only then can we be whole—
United mind, and flesh, and soul.

Our mental and physical states are not separate—they exist in profound and constant dialogue. Every thought we think and every emotion we feel carries energy. When we suppress these internal experiences—especially the difficult or painful ones—

they don't simply disappear. Instead, they find another outlet: the body.

The phrase *"What the mind suppresses, the body expresses"* reflects this intimate relationship between mind and body. Suppressed emotions—grief, fear, anger, shame—often surface through physical symptoms: muscle tension, digestive issues, headaches, fatigue, insomnia, autoimmune conditions, or inexplicable chronic pain. These are not random ailments; they are somatic messages from within, alerting us that something has gone unacknowledged, something requires our attention.

This is particularly evident in the aftermath of trauma. The body, unable to cognitively process overwhelming experiences, stores them in the form of sensory memory. Without resolution, these stored impressions become energetic blockages—echoes of the unspoken and unfelt. Renowned therapeutic methods like the *Hoffman Process* are grounded in this awareness, emphasizing that healing occurs not only through intellectual understanding but also through emotional release and bodily integration.

At its core, energy is neutral—neither good nor bad. But when we attach our thoughts to emotion, that energy becomes polarized. Positive thoughts raise our vibrational frequency; negative thoughts lower it, creating emotional density that affects our state of being. Left unprocessed, this dense emotional energy embeds itself into our physical and energetic systems. Over time, it can manifest as recurring life patterns, health conditions, or emotional triggers.

Many of these patterns originate from a false sense of self—one shaped by inherited beliefs, cultural conditioning, and rigid societal expectations. We internalize ideals that often do not reflect our unique essence. In an attempt to conform, we suppress authentic thoughts and feelings that challenge the status quo. With repetition, this suppression moves from conscious denial to subconscious repression. What starts as personal dissonance eventually becomes collective dysfunction—unresolved wounds passed down through generations as inherited trauma.

And yet, the body remembers.

It remembers the unshed tears of our ancestors.

It remembers the silenced cries of our inner child.

It remembers the stories that were never allowed to be told.

These silent burdens do not vanish; they live within us—expressed through posture, breath, fatigue, or illness. But they also offer a portal to healing. Through somatic awareness, emotional honesty, mindfulness, and spiritual practices, we begin to unravel these layered imprints. By recognizing the body as a sacred messenger, we give ourselves permission to feel, to release, and ultimately—to transform.

The spiritually awakened soul understands this well. Rather than resisting pain or clinging to the past, it embraces the alchemy of letting go. It learns to forgive—not just others, but itself. It becomes a blank slate, a fertile womb for renewal. In surrendering what no longer serves, the soul makes space for truth to emerge—for potentiality to unfold.

Reflective Conclusion

A Call to Integration

What the mind suppresses, the body expresses is not merely a psychological observation—it is a spiritual truth. Healing begins the moment we stop bypassing our discomfort and start listening to the wisdom of the body. Our pain holds intelligence. Our symptoms are signals. When we courageously face what we've buried, we break free from cycles of suppression, illness, and inherited trauma. We liberate not only ourselves but the generations before and after us.

The path to wholeness demands we bridge the gap between mind and body, between past and present, between knowing and feeling. In doing so, we reclaim our power—not by resisting what arises, but by allowing it to guide us home.

Chapter 40

Silence: Not the Absence of Sound, but the Presence of the Divine

In hush of dawn or twilight's grace,
No voice is heard yet fills the space.
A sacred calm, so vast, so wide—
Where ego fades and truths reside.

Not void, but full—a whispered flame,
Where soul and Source become the same.
No need for words, no need to strive—
For in pure silence, God's alive.

In a world saturated with noise and distractions, silence has become not only a rare commodity but a deeply essential state of being. The constant barrage of external noise—from conversations, media, traffic, and technology—has been normalized to the point that many of us feel uncomfortable without it. Yet, what often goes unnoticed is the even louder internal noise: the relentless stream of thoughts, emotions, worries, and mental chatter that keeps our minds in a state of unrest.

Many people have grown so accustomed to this mental and environmental clamor that silence feels unsettling. It threatens the illusion of control and stability. When we are alone in silence, we often encounter the very thoughts and feelings we've tried to suppress. This confrontation can feel like impending doom, when in truth, it is an invitation—an invitation to meet the self and the Divine.

Silence is not a void or emptiness. Rather, it is a sacred space—a threshold into stillness where the noise of the world fades and the soul begins to speak. In silence, the mind quiets, and in that quiet, we begin to hear something deeper: the whisper of inner wisdom, the subtle guidance of the divine, the presence of something greater than ourselves.

Across spiritual traditions, silence is revered as a pathway to self-awareness and divine communion. In Christianity, it is used as a mode of prayer and listening, a way to discern God's voice. In Buddhism, silence is a vehicle for meditation and awakening, where stillness reveals the impermanence and interconnection of all things. In Hinduism, *Mauna*—the discipline of silence—is seen as a gateway to inner peace and union with Absolute Reality. Judaism values silence as a sacred space for reflection and divine encounter, while in Islam, silence from unnecessary or harmful speech is considered a virtuous path to spiritual refinement.

Silence serves both as a shield and a mirror. It shields us from the over-stimulation of the world and mirrors back our innermost truths. By reducing both external and internal distractions, it offers a serene landscape for inner clarity and insight. In that clarity, we begin to see our thoughts for what they are—transient—and become more attuned to what lies beneath them: the eternal presence of the Divine.

More than just a tool for reflection, silence is itself a form of spiritual expression. It is often described as the "language of

God." In Catholic symbolism, the empty tomb is a silent proclamation of resurrection and hope. In contemplative practices, it is believed that God often speaks not through thunderous declarations but through the "still, small voice" found in silence.

To embrace silence is to step into sacred communion. It is where the soul sheds its distractions, where the ego dissolves, and where the self becomes receptive to the presence that permeates all life. It is not the absence of sound, but the presence of depth. It is where revelation is born—not through noise, but through the quiet unfolding of spiritual truth.

Reflective Conclusion

In the fast-paced chaos of modern life, reclaiming silence is an act of spiritual rebellion—and renewal. It is in silence that we reconnect with our innermost being, restore our spiritual alignment, and reestablish communion with the Divine. Silence invites us to listen—not with our ears, but with our soul.

Understanding that **silence is not the absence of sound but the presence of the Divine** transforms how we engage with it. It is not something to fear or fill, but something to honor and enter. In its quietude, we find not emptiness, but the fullness of presence, peace, and purpose. Cultivating moments of silence is not only a spiritual practice—it is a sacred necessity for anyone seeking depth, truth, and divine connection in a noisy world.

Chapter 41

Alone but Not Lonely

In quiet stillness, I find my grace,
No need for crowds, no frantic pace.
The world may fade, yet I remain—
A soul at peace, beyond the pain.

No grasp for hands, no search for eyes,
For in my heart, the cosmos lies.
Though none may walk this path I tread,
I'm not alone—I'm Spirit-led.

In sacred hush, I hear the tone—
The universe sings, and I've come home.
Solitude blooms where fear once grew,
Alone, yet whole—complete, and true.

Human beings are inherently social creatures, engaging in constant interaction with others as we navigate the various dimensions of life. Through these interactions, we co-create experiences and share ourselves in relationships of every kind—casual acquaintances, professional alliances, familial ties, friendships, and intimate soul connections. Each encounter serves a purpose, some fleeting-like whispers in time, others enduring like steady flames meant to walk beside us until our final breath.

Within the framework of these relationships, we begin to define ourselves. Our roles, responsibilities, and even our worth often become entangled in the narratives we build with others. These connections, while meaningful and fulfilling, can also act as invisible tethers—anchors that keep us grounded in a shared reality. At times, they serve as shields, buffering us from the storms of life. And yet, they can also obscure the deeper truth of who we are beyond all identities and roles.

We often fear being alone because we equate it with loneliness—an uncomfortable state of separation that makes us feel exposed and insignificant. But this fear is rooted in illusion. There comes a crucial turning point in every soul's journey when these attachments must be gently loosened. This unraveling is not abandonment, but an invitation. It is the soul's call to return inward, to shed the noise of the external world and attune to the quiet hum of the universe pulsing within.

In this sacred solitude, we are not being punished—we are being prepared. The isolation, though uncomfortable at first, becomes a crucible for transformation. Without the distractions and validations of the external world, we learn to hear the whispers of our inner voice. We begin to recognize ourselves not as fragments defined by relationships, but as whole, sovereign beings—vibrational expressions of life itself.

This phase of being alone is essential. It is the gateway to awakening dormant potentials and unleashing the immense creative force that resides within. As this inner power stirs, we evolve into conscious creators—master builders of our own realm, capable of shaping reality through clarity, intention, and alignment. No longer tethered to the limitations of the physical dimension, we experience an expanded consciousness that reaches beyond the constraints of this three-dimensional construct.

Eventually, solitude is no longer perceived as a prison but embraced as a sanctuary. It becomes a meditative space where the soul can rest, reflect, and realign with its true essence. In this space, we feel connected—not to people or places, but to *all that is*. The soul learns to dance in the silence, to commune with the Divine, and to feel the presence of something infinitely vast and unconditionally loving.

To be "alone but not lonely" is to discover the profound distinction between physical separation and spiritual connection. Solitude is simply the absence of others, while loneliness is the absence of connection—to self, to source, to meaning. One can be surrounded by people and feel utterly alone or be physically isolated and feel divinely accompanied.

Reflective Conclusion

In the end, the path of solitude is not a detour from the journey—it is the journey. It is the sacred space where illusions fall away, and truth is revealed. To be alone but not lonely is to embody the knowing that we are never truly separate. It is to stand in stillness and recognize that within the vast quiet, there is a presence—ever constant, ever loving, ever whole. And from this wholeness, we find the courage to walk our path, not in fear, but in faith—deeply connected to the infinite, even in silence.

Chapter 42

Be Simple but Not Ordinary

Be simple—like the morning light,
That gently breaks the grip of night.
No need for thunder, flame, or show—
Just grace in every quiet glow.

Be not so ordinary, though,
That you forget your soul's true flow.
Let every step, though soft and still,
Reflect divine and sacred will.

In silent acts, let truth be seen—
In humble ways, remain serene.
For in a world that craves the loud,
The gentle heart stands most unbowed.

Simplicity, at its core, refers to the state of being clear, natural, and easy to understand. It reflects coherence, where thoughts and actions align with consistency and logic. Yet beyond its surface definition, simplicity holds a deeper spiritual significance—one that invites us to return to what truly matters.

In a spiritual sense, simplicity is not the absence of ambition or richness, but the presence of purpose and inner clarity. It is a conscious stripping away of the excess—material possessions, needless distractions, false identities, and rigid beliefs—to create space for what is essential: our relationship with the Divine. It is not about deprivation, but liberation. By releasing the burdens that clutter our minds and lives, we allow the soul to breathe, to dwell in presence, and to hear the quiet voice of Spirit that often gets drowned in the noise of modern existence.

Simplicity begins within the heart. It reflects contentment, not complacency, depth, not denial. It is nurtured by practices such as prayer, contemplation, and surrender. As we simplify our inner landscape, our outer lives follow—becoming less chaotic, more intentional, and more reflective of a life attuned to higher purpose.

Yet to be *simple* does not mean to be *ordinary.*

Ordinariness, often viewed through a cultural lens, implies lack of distinction or uniqueness. In a world driven by ego, performance, and validation, being labeled ordinary is often met with discomfort. We are conditioned to crave exceptionalism—to be seen, applauded, and validated. As a result, many craft elaborate identities and seek external markers of worth, creating illusions that mask their true nature.

But in spiritual truth, ordinariness is not something to fear. It is, paradoxically, the gateway to the extraordinary. To be spiritually "ordinary" is to live authentically, embracing who we truly are without masks or pretense. It is to see God in the simple rhythms of life—in work, in family, in stillness, and in service. It is to stop chasing grandeur and instead awaken to the sacredness already present in each moment.

Living a spiritually ordinary life does not mean mediocrity—it means humility, integrity, and presence. It is a life of quiet power, where one no longer needs to perform or compare, but rather contributes with grace and purpose. Such ordinariness becomes an offering—simple yet profound, unseen yet eternal.

Thus, to *be simple but not ordinary* is to embody a life that is unburdened yet luminous. It means living with clarity and ease, while retaining one's distinct essence and depth. It is the art of embracing the humble without losing the holy, of walking lightly without becoming lost, and of living deeply without needing to dazzle.

Reflective Conclusion

In a world obsessed with complexity, appearance, and acclaim, choosing simplicity is a radical act. Choosing to be authentic rather than impressive is a return to soul. When we embrace simplicity without succumbing to blandness—and ordinariness without losing uniqueness—we uncover a sacred balance.

To be simple but not ordinary is to live from essence rather than ego, from truth rather than performance. It is to discover that greatness often comes clothed in humility, and that the divine is often revealed in the mundane. In the quiet spaces of life, where simplicity meets soul, we remember who we truly are not here to impress, but to express the light within.

Chapter 43

Death Is Not the End Just a Shift in Form

Death is not the end we fear,
But just a shift from here to here.
A soul set free from form and name,
Still burning with eternal flame.

The body fades, but not the light,
We journey onward, out of sight.
From one brief life, the soul takes flight—
Into new dawns, beyond the night.

Though gone from touch, they're not apart,
They live within the beating heart.
Love does not die—it simply grows,
In unseen ways the spirit knows.

We often mourn death because we see it as the end of everything we know and love. Our attachments—to identities, relationships, accomplishments, and possessions—bind us to the illusion that this physical life is all there is. Though we may resent aging or the limitations it imposes, many would still choose to extend life indefinitely if given the chance. A beautiful life, after all, is hard to let go.

Yet beneath the veil of time and form lies a deeper truth: we are eternal beings, temporarily experiencing a finite dimension of reality. Death is not the annihilation of self but a transition—a shift in form, not in essence. This life may be one projection of the soul among countless others, all unfolding in parallel timelines or layered dimensions. At moments, we may even glimpse these layers through phenomena like *déjà vu*—the eerie sense of having lived this moment before—or *jamais vu*, when the familiar suddenly feels foreign. These sensations hint at a deeper entanglement of soul experiences beyond linear time.

Modern psychology and neurology have identified a range of memory phenomena tied to these feelings—such as *déjà vécu* (the sensation of re-living an experience), *déjà rêvé* (the feeling that a moment was previously dreamed), or *déjà senti* (the familiarity of a sensory feeling). While science searches for neurological explanations, spiritually inclined traditions view such moments as bleed-throughs from other lifetimes or soul memories surfacing in our awareness.

Beyond individual experiences, cultural traditions across the globe offer diverse interpretations of death. While some see it as an end, many view it as a passage.

Spiritual and Cultural Views on Death:

- **Christianity** teaches that the soul faces judgment and enters either eternal reward or punishment.
- **Islam** holds that souls are accountable for their earthly deeds, with paradise or hell as their destination.

- **Buddhism** and **Hinduism** embrace the cyclical nature of life through reincarnation, where the soul continues evolving through successive lifetimes.
- **Indigenous cultures** across Africa, the Americas, and Asia often believe the dead remain spiritually active—guiding and protecting the living.

These beliefs affirm a common understanding: that the soul transcends death, and life does not cease with the end of physical form. Death, in this light, is not a disappearance but a metamorphosis—a soul transitioning into new dimensions of experience.

This truth is celebrated in rituals around the world:

- In **Mexico**, *Día de los Muertos* welcomes departed souls back into the lives of the living with joy, color, and reverence.
- **Chinese** and **Japanese** traditions emphasize ancestral veneration and maintaining harmony with those who have passed on.
- In **Hinduism**, cremation rituals and the scattering of ashes in sacred rivers reflect the return of the soul to divine origins.
- **African** cultures uphold the presence of ancestors as active members of the community, linking the living and the dead.

In contrast, **modern Western societies** often approach death with avoidance or denial—treating it as a medical failure rather than a sacred transition. This detachment can make grief more difficult to process and strips the passage of death of its spiritual significance. Earlier Western periods, such as the **Victorian era**, at least acknowledged death with symbolic mourning and ritual, giving space for emotional and communal processing.

The biblical text of *Ecclesiastes* reminds us of death's inevitability. It portrays mortality as the great equalizer, suggesting that our earthly pursuits are fleeting and that memory fades. But from a soul-centered perspective, this ephemerality applies only to form, not essence.

Reflective Conclusion

Embracing the Shift, Not the End

While death appears to be a finality to those rooted in the material world, it is, in truth, merely the closing of one chapter in the soul's eternal story. The body may return to dust, but the soul continues on, enriched by the lessons and love experienced in this lifetime. Life, death, and rebirth form an eternal spiral of becoming.

From this lens, we can begin to see death not as something to fear, but as a sacred unfolding—part of the soul's divine curriculum. We honor those who have transitioned not by clinging to sorrow, but by celebrating the unique imprint they've left in our hearts. For though they no longer walk beside us in form, they live within us—integrated aspects of the same divine consciousness, forever connected in the oneness of being.

Death, then, is not the end—it is a sacred return, a soul's reminder that love transcends form, and that life, in its essence, never truly ceases.

Chapter 44

Life Between Lives: A Journey Beyond the Veil

Between the breaths of birth and death,
A silent realm, a soul's true depth.
Not bound by time, nor form, nor name,
Yet every life, it fans the flame.

We meet our guides, review the past,
Choose lessons deep, and roles recast.
In light we plan, with love we weave,
The journeys we are yet to leave.

So, fear not death, nor mourn the end—
Each life a loop, and time a friend.

Some believe that there is more to life than what we perceive through our physical senses. That beyond birth and death lies a continuum—a vast, unseen realm where the soul journeys, learns, and evolves. This concept, often referred to as Life Between Lives (LBL), explores the spiritual existence that occurs in the space between incarnations.

Life Between Lives spirituality was popularized by Dr. Michael Newton, a hypnotherapist whose pioneering work in spiritual regression uncovered detailed accounts of what happens to souls in the non-physical realm. Through deep hypnosis, clients accessed memories not only of past lives but of the inter-life period—the state of being when the soul is no longer in a physical body yet not fully incarnated into a new one. This profound work has shed light on the hidden tapestry of the soul's journey.

The Inter-Life Realm

According to Newton's findings, in this inter-life realm, souls exist as pure energetic beings. This space is not merely a resting place, but a sacred school of learning, healing, and preparation.

Through spiritual regression, individuals are guided into a deep meditative or hypnotic state where they can access memories of this non-physical existence. In these sessions, many report:

- **Meeting Spiritual Guides** who offer insight, comfort, and wisdom.
- **Reuniting with Soul Groups**, kindred spirits who journey through multiple lifetimes together, often shifting roles—parent, child, friend, lover—across incarnations.
- **Life Reviews**, in which the soul, with loving guidance, reflects on lessons from its most recent life.
- **Encounters with a Soul Council**, a group of wise, evolved beings who help the soul evaluate its growth and prepare for future incarnations.

- **Planning Future Lives**, where souls may choose the circumstances, challenges, and relationships of their next life in alignment with their spiritual objectives.

These experiences are not dogmatic claims but deeply personal, transformative recollections that often carry emotional and spiritual weight for those who undergo them.

The Purpose of Life Between Lives Work

The exploration of the life between lives realm provides individuals with more than just curiosity-satisfying answers; it offers meaningful benefits, such as:

- **Emotional Healing** – Understanding the spiritual roots of present-life challenges can lead to deep psychological release.
- **Expanded Awareness** – Gaining insight into the soul's broader journey fosters a sense of continuity and belonging in the universe.
- **Clarified Purpose** – Connecting with one's soul mission and life blueprint can lead to a more focused, meaningful existence.
- **Spiritual Reconnection** – Many reports feeling reconnected to Source, to their higher self, and to the greater spiritual order that governs life.

In essence, LBL work invites a profound reorientation of how we view ourselves—not just as physical beings moving linearly through time, but as eternal souls participating in a grand evolutionary spiral.

Complementary Teachings: Dolores Cannon's Legacy

In essence, LBL work invites a profound reorientation of how we view ourselves—not just as physical beings moving linearly through time, but as eternal souls participating in a grand evolutionary spiral.

Dolores Cannon, a trailblazer in past-life regression and quantum healing hypnosis, contributed greatly to our understanding of the afterlife and reincarnation. Her work mirrors many of the themes found in Newton's research but adds additional layers of metaphysical and multidimensional insight.

In books like *Between Death and Life*, Cannon shares thousands of regression sessions in which clients recount experiences in the afterlife—stages of soul review, healing, planning, and encounters with spiritual beings. Her work affirms the cyclical nature of life and the soul's continual journey through various incarnations.

She emphasized:

- **Life After Death** – Death is not an end but a transition. The soul moves into a spirit realm for reflection and rejuvenation.
- **Reincarnation** – Souls return to physical life repeatedly, each time with new roles, challenges, and opportunities for growth.
- **The Spirit Realm** – This intermediate space is a

realm of profound love, intelligence, and learning—where souls connect with guides, other beings, and their own higher wisdom.

- **Purpose and Free Will** – While souls plan their next lives, they retain free will. Life on Earth is both a school and a co-creative playground for soul evolution.

Cannon's research also suggests that we willingly forget our past lives upon reincarnation to fully immerse ourselves in the present experience. However, the memories remain accessible at a soul level and can be retrieved when the timing is right—often when we are ready to remember who we truly are.

Reflective Conclusion

A Soul's Eternal Journey

The exploration of *Life Between Lives* is not merely an esoteric curiosity—it is a deeply healing and awakening journey into the essence of who we are. These teachings remind us that we are not random accidents of biology, nor are we defined solely by our current identities or experiences.

We are souls—eternal, evolving, and intricately woven into the divine fabric of the cosmos.

When we view life from this expanded lens, pain gains context, relationships become sacred contracts, and each moment becomes a thread in a much greater tapestry. Our struggles are not punishments, but curriculum. Our gifts are not just talents, but tools chosen for a mission.

Whether one embraces these views as literal truth or symbolic metaphor, the invitation remains the same: to live with greater awareness, compassion, and reverence for the sacred journey we are all on.

And perhaps most beautifully, to remember—beyond the roles we play, the stories we live, and the bodies we inhabit—we are luminous beings, guided by love, on a path home to ourselves.

Chapter 45

Parallel Lives: Exploring the Multidimensional Self

In dreams I walk a different way,
A path I almost took one day.
Another self with different eyes,
Still searching truth beneath the skies.

A mirrored life, a silent thread,
Where words unsaid are softly said.
We're branches of the same old tree,
Each leaf a note in destiny.

Across the veil, I sometimes see—
The quiet whisper: "I am thee."

In spiritual philosophy, the idea of *parallel lives* proposes that we may exist not as a single identity bound to one timeline, but as multiple versions of ourselves—living out different outcomes, shaped by different choices, across alternate realities. This concept, while mystical, intersects with both metaphysical teachings and quantum theories, offering a compelling lens through which to explore the nature of consciousness and possibility.

The idea is simple yet profound: each choice we make spawns a new path. While we consciously walk one, others may unfold in parallel dimensions—realms where different "you" exist, making alternate decisions, learning different lessons, and experiencing other variations of life. These parallel selves aren't just abstractions. Some spiritual traditions suggest we can access and learn from them.

Key Concepts of Parallel Lives

- **Multiple Realities:** The foundational idea behind parallel lives is that the universe—or perhaps multiverse—contains countless dimensions, each representing a unique outcome of our choices. These realities coexist, unseen, but no less real.
- **Spiritual Exploration:** Practices like meditation, dreamwork, Reiki, and deep journaling are believed to offer glimpses into these parallel timelines. Vivid dreams, déjà vu, or moments of inexplicable clarity may be echoes from another version of ourselves.
- **Learning and Growth:** By connecting with these other selves, we may gain insights, heal emotional wounds, and accelerate our growth. A soul navigating diverse paths gains broader wisdom than one confined to a single track.
- **Interconnectedness:** Parallel lives emphasize the web of interconnection—not only between beings, but within our multidimensional selves. Actions in one reality may ripple across others in mysterious and subtle ways.

Spiritual and Scientific Crossroads

While the concept of parallel lives is largely metaphysical, modern science—particularly **quantum physics**—offers intriguing parallels.

- **Many-Worlds Interpretation:** This theory in quantum mechanics proposes that every quantum event causes the universe to split, creating separate branches where all possible outcomes occur. Each of these branches can be thought of as a "parallel life."
- **Superposition:** In quantum theory, particles can exist in multiple states simultaneously until observed. This idea has become a metaphor in personal development, suggesting we, too, exist in many potential states, waiting to be "collapsed" by our focus and intention.
- **Entanglement:** Just as entangled particles affect one another across great distances, the soul's parallel lives may be energetically connected—each version influencing and informing the other.
- **Observer Effect:** Quantum physics suggests that the act of observation alters the outcome of an event. This principle is often interpreted spiritually to mean that where we place our attention shapes the reality we experience.

Applications in Personal Development

Drawing inspiration from these quantum concepts, many spiritual teachers and coaches have developed tools to help individuals explore and embody their parallel potentials:

- **Quantum Visualization:** A meditative technique in which one envisions an ideal version of themselves in a parallel timeline, aligning with that reality through emotion and intent.
- **Reality Selection Meditation:** This practice helps individuals consciously "choose" which path they wish to align with by shifting thoughts, beliefs, and frequencies to match that version of reality.
- **Parallel Selves as Archetypes:** Some see parallel lives as symbolic expressions of potential selves—each representing a version of you that took a different route. Integrating aspects of these selves can lead to healing, confidence, and empowerment.
- **Exploring Regret and Forgiveness:** By contemplating the lives we *could* have lived, we often gain compassion for our current path. We see not failure, but sacred choice. We understand that each path—taken or not—serves the soul's evolution.

Spiritual Traditions That Touch Upon Parallel Lives

- **Hinduism**: Concepts like karma, reincarnation, and multiple universes offer frameworks for understanding the coexistence of many lives and realities. Time is not linear but cyclical.
- **Mystical Judaism and Kabbalah**: These traditions speak of layered dimensions and soul fragments that incarnate in different ways across time and space.
- **Modern Mysticism and Energy Healing**: Modalities like quantum healing and shamanic journeying often speak of timelines, parallel existences, and soul retrieval—accessing lost or alternate aspects of oneself.

A Note on Discernment

It's important to distinguish between theoretical models in physics—like the parallel lives model or many-worlds interpretation—and the metaphorical use of these ideas in spiritual and personal development contexts. While physics seeks to explain the fabric of the universe through observation and math, spirituality uses these concepts to guide inner transformation and intuitive exploration.

The value in this metaphor lies not in scientific proof, but in the invitation it offers: to live more consciously, to explore what's possible, and to acknowledge the vast, multidimensional nature of the self.

Reflective Conclusion

The Self Beyond One Story

The idea of parallel lives invites us to loosen our grip on the singular identity we think defines us. It encourages humility in the face of the infinite and possibility in the face of limitation.

Who might you have become if you'd taken a different path? What parts of you remain dormant, waiting to be awakened? And what wisdom might another version of you—walking a different journey—have to share with the one reading these words now?

Perhaps you are not one person but many. A kaleidoscope of potentials, layered and luminous, orbiting around a singular soul.

And maybe, just maybe, in quiet moments of insight, imagination, or déjà vu, you've already met yourself—across the veil of time, across the bend of probability, reminding you that all paths, all choices, are part of the wholeness you truly are.

Chapter 46

Return to Oneness

We came as drops from sacred sea,
To learn, to grow, to simply be.
In form we wandered, lost in name,
Yet deep inside, we're still the same.

The stars remember, so do the trees,
The silent truth rides on the breeze.
No walls remain when love is near,
All things dissolve; the path is clear.

Return, dear soul, to what you knew—
The light, the Source, the timeless you.

In the spiritual journey, *returning to oneness* is not about going somewhere new—rather, it is a process of remembering who we already are. It is a return to the fundamental truth that we are not separate but intricately connected to all that exists. It is the dissolution of illusion, the stripping away of egoic boundaries, and the merging once more with the sacred Source from which we came.

This principle of oneness is echoed in many spiritual traditions—from ancient Eastern philosophies to mystical branches of the Abrahamic religions—and is increasingly emphasized in modern spiritual teachings. Regardless of the language used or the practices followed, the core essence remains the same: the realization that separation is illusion and unity is truth.

Core Concepts of Oneness

Unity and Interconnectedness

At the heart of this teaching is the understanding that all life is interconnected. Every being, every atom, and every phenomenon is part of a unified field of consciousness. What affects one, affects all. The illusion of separateness dissolves in the light of awareness, revealing the tapestry of unity that weaves through all things.

Dissolution of the Ego

The ego, in its limited role, creates the false narrative of separation. It defines "me" and "mine," erecting boundaries that fracture our perception of the whole. To return to oneness, the ego must be lovingly softened—not destroyed but transcended—so that the soul can remember its infinite nature.

Transcending Duality

Oneness transcends the binaries of right and wrong, good and bad, self and other. It exists beyond judgment and categorization. In this space, opposites are integrated rather than opposed, and everything is seen as part of a greater unfolding.

Realization of True Nature

This journey is ultimately about remembering our true essence. We are not merely bodies or identities—we are eternal consciousness experiencing itself through form. To awaken to this truth is to awaken to oneness itself.

Pathways Back to Oneness

1. Spiritual Practices

Mindfulness, meditation, breathwork, and yoga are tools that quiet the noise of the mind and help us reconnect with the stillness at our core. In that stillness, the illusion of separation falls away.

2. Cultivating Love and Compassion

When we extend love without condition and practice compassion without judgment, we begin to see ourselves in others. Through this lens, we no longer see separation—we see reflections.

3. Shifting Perspective

True unity is experienced when we release the idea of gain or loss, success or failure. From a neutral and expanded perspective, life is seen as a flow of experiences, not as a ledger of outcomes.

4. Practicing Gratitude

Gratitude shifts our focus from what is lacking to what is present. It awakens us to the web of interdependence that supports our existence and softens the walls of isolation built by the ego.

5. Communion with Nature

Nature reminds us of our place in the great whole. The trees, oceans, skies, and creatures all operate in harmony, guided by the intelligence of the universe. When we align with this rhythm, we feel our oneness with all life.

Oneness in Different Traditions

Hinduism

The ancient Vedic teachings center around *Brahman*, the ultimate reality that permeates all existence. The realization that *Atman* (the individual soul) is not separate from *Brahman* is the core of spiritual awakening in Hinduism.

Islam

In Islam, *Tawhid* refers to the oneness of God. This profound principle shapes the believer's worldview—reminding them that all aspects of life are expressions of divine unity. There is no true power or existence but that of the One.

Modern Spiritual Philosophies

Contemporary spiritual teachings emphasize that oneness is not a belief, but a lived experience. Through presence, introspection, energy work, and mindful awareness, we begin to directly experience the unity that underlies all things.

The Drop and the Ocean

Oneness is not a destination—it is our origin and our nature.

We are like a drop of water that once separated from the

infinite ocean of consciousness. Yet within that single drop exists the whole—the depth, the essence, the memory of the ocean itself.

When that drop remembers, when it dissolves back into the vast sea, there is no longer distinction between drop and ocean. There is only wholeness. There is only One.

Reflective Conclusion

The Sacred Return

Returning to oneness is not about acquiring something new; it is about letting go. Letting go of the layers that veil the truth. Letting go of the narratives that confine us. Letting go of the illusion of being separate from the Source that breathes life into all things.

This return is a sacred homecoming. A reunion not only with the Divine, but with the fullness of who we are. When we embrace this unity, we begin to live from love instead of fear, from wisdom instead of worry, from connection instead of isolation.

In this space of oneness, the soul finds peace.

In this space of oneness, the heart remembers.

In this space of oneness… we become whole again.

You Are Not the Ego, But the Divine Spark Within

You are not the voice that fears,
Nor the mind that doubts and hides.
You are not the mask it wears,
But the truth the soul provides.

You are not the pride that boasts,
Nor the wound that seeks to win.
You are not the fleeting ghost,
But the light that burns within.

You are not the roles you play,
Or the names the world assigns.
You are more than flesh and clay—
You are soul beyond all lines.

You are not the weight of past,
Or the future steeped in haze.
You are presence, free and vast,
Guided by eternal rays.

You are not the fear of lack,
Nor the need to chase or prove.
You are love that draws life back,
In a silent, sacred groove.

You are not what others see,
Or the storm that stirs the skin.
You are stillness, wild and free—
The Divine Spark deep within.

So, when ego cries out loud,
Let your spirit softly grin.
For behind the noisy crowd,
God's own whisper lies within.

MysticSojourn66

Beyond the Veil

Behind the mask, beyond the veil,
The soul redeems, itself reclaims.
Through tears and pain, it softly stirs,
Revealed through hope, released from hurt.

Though at first, confusion looms,
Resistance fades, and clarity blooms.
Life's not against you, but for you still—
Realize this, and joy will fill.

Duality is the game we play,
Our choices shown in full display.
Entrapped by either end, we stray,
Submitting to ego's bold dismay.

But alas, the soul awakens—bright—
With truth revealed, it shakes this life.
Limited thoughts now left behind,
The once-obscured light redefined.

A still, small voice begins to sing,
Beyond the noise, a gentle ring.
It whispers not of who you've been,
But of the light that dwells within.

So let that light illuminate,
And patiently for grace await.
With clarity, illusion ends—
The soul, at last, transcends, ascends.

MysticSojourn66

About the Author

Arwin Valencia, MD is a board-certified pediatrician with specialized training in Neonatology. He earned his medical degree from the University of Santo Tomas, completed his pediatric residency at Richmond University Medical Center, and pursued fellowship training in Neonatal-Perinatal Medicine at the University of California, Irvine.

Dr. Valencia has authored and co-authored numerous peer-reviewed publications in neonatal medicine, with a particular focus on preterm infants and the complex conditions affecting their development. His research, spanning both clinical and translational domains, continues to inform and advance neonatal care. His work is widely cited, underscoring his active contribution to the scientific community.

Beyond the walls of the NICU, Dr. Valencia is a lifelong seeker of wisdom—both scientific and spiritual. His journey bridges modern medicine with metaphysical understanding, uniting the analytical mind with the intuitive heart. Rooted in a belief that true healing arises from the integration of body, mind, and soul, he advocates for a more holistic approach to health—one grounded in self-awareness, compassion, and conscious living.

A devoted student of ancient traditions and sacred texts, he draws inspiration from the poetic works of Rumi, Hafez, Gibran, Ferdowsi, and even the mythopoetic tales of Tolkien. His interests also span ancient civilizations, quantum physics, Jungian psychology, Hermetic principles, The Law of One,

Stoic philosophy, Buddhism, and mystical teachings across Kabbalistic and Abrahamic traditions.

Through his writings, Dr. Valencia invites readers on a soulful journey of remembrance—to reconnect with the divine spark within and allow its light to illuminate the path toward healing, wholeness, and purpose.

www.ingramcontent.com/pod-product-compliance
Lightning Source LLC
LaVergne TN
LVHW090935080826
845145LV00003B/754

* 9 7 8 1 9 6 6 8 3 7 2 2 0 *